Angels at Pincher Creek

And 31 Other True Stories About God's Providential Care

Selected by Mabel Tupper

World rights reserved. This book or any portion thereof may not be copied or reproduced in any form or manner whatever, except as provided by law, without the written permission of the publisher, except by a reviewer who may quote brief passages in a review.

The author assumes full responsibility for the accuracy of all facts and quotations as cited in this book. The opinions expressed in this book are the author's personal views and interpretations, and do not necessarily reflect those of the publisher.

This book is provided with the understanding that the publisher is not engaged in giving spiritual, legal, medical, or other professional advice. If authoritative advice is needed, the reader should seek the counsel of a competent professional.

Copyright © 2014 TEACH Services, Inc.
ISBN-13: 978-1-4796-0075-5 (Paperback)
ISBN-13: 978-1-4796-0076-2 (ePub)
ISBN-13: 978-1-4796-0077-9 (Mobi)
Library of Congress Control Number: 2013956415

Published by

Foreword

The compiler of this collection of thrilling stories has spent years gathering them. Here you will find evidence of angels coming to the rescue of literature evangelists while they went from door to door, and giving them protection from dangerous dogs and savage men. Angels are not above doing a humble chore. As you read on, you will learn of an angel who filled a wood box to keep a helpless woman from freezing to death in the far North.

Reading these experiences will convince you that Heaven is interested in caring for weak, erring humans. Your faith in God will be strengthened as His love and care will be made manifest.

Laverne Tucker
Former President of the Quiet Hour

Preface

"The angel of the Lord encampeth round about them that fear him, and delivereth them" (Ps. 34:7).

I began collecting the stories for this book after hearing the powerful testimonies of two different colporteurs (literature evangelists who go door to door selling religious books and magazines) who received help from angels, in their times of need. These workers for the Lord told their stories to me personally, and those stories changed the course of my life.

The first story to move my heart so powerfully was told to me in Calgary, Alberta, Canada, in the early winter of 1926. Attending a colporteur convention for the first time, it was my good fortune to room with a dear, experienced, elderly woman colporteur. In the evening, when it was time to sleep, we talked about the events of the day. "Let me tell you what happened to me just before I left Pincher Creek to come to Calgary," my roommate began. And thus was born the story, "Angels at Pincher Creek."

When the colporteur convention was over, we all went to our homes, and then on to our fields of labor. But this little story always stayed with me, and became a strong influence in my life. I had grown up in the home of people who belonged to another denomination, and while I fully believed the Bible stories of angels appearing to human beings, I had assumed that the miracles related in the Bible were unique for that time. I thought that God did not directly intervene in our lives like that anymore.

The story of Pincher Creek, having happened about a week before the convention, showed me that God does work in today's world as of old. It started me on a search for stories of the providential hand of God as revealed in the lives of people today.

Nearly twenty years later, in Placerville, California, I heard the second story, "Unexpected Rescue."

Since then, I have collected stories of angels' visits, and of instantaneous healings that could not be explained except by the supernatural hand of God. There are other stories that verify the passage, "By his light I walked through darkness" (Job 29:3). God led the people of Israel through the desert with a pillar of fire by night and a cloud during the day. God still uses His light in a similar way to lead people today. The stories of several people who had such an experience document this fact.

Christians all over the world have reported incidents where angels appeared to their enemies as guards, saving them from harm. Many of these stories come from missionaries during the last 200 years. Such a story called "Where are the Watchmen," told by W. A Spicer in his book, *The Hand That Intervenes,* (copyright 1918) is typical.

Another category of stories that have come to me includes experiences with dreams. "For God speaketh once, yea twice, yet man perceiveth it not. In a dream, in a vision of the night, when deep sleep falleth upon men, in slumberings upon the bed (Job 33:14, 15).

From Genesis through the New Testament God has given instructions through dreams. He gave dreams to Abraham, Jacob, Laban, and others. In the New Testament a dream instructed Joseph, the wise men, Cornelius and Peter. Ananias was given instruction about Saul in a dream while the newly converted disciple was fasting and praying in Damascus. In the book of Acts we find these prophetic words, originally spoken by the prophet Joel. "And it shall come to pass in the last days, saith God… your sons and your daughters shall prophesy, and your young men shall see visions, and your old men shall dream dreams" (Acts 2:17).

Today people are led by dreams in different places, but we always must test these alleged revelations by the written Word of God and by the fruits that result. We cannot follow dreams that are contrary to the Bible. I have heard and read of many vivid, meaningful dreams in our day. A number of them are presented here.

The power of prayer is the topic of many of the stories I have received over the years. "O taste and see that the Lord is good: blessed is the man that trusteth in him" (Ps. 34:8), is the theme of these stories. When Jesus was here on earth He promised that those who seek God in faith will have their prayers answered according to God's will. Those who walk with the Lord in the Spirit and are led by Him, will pray as Christ prayed: "If thou be willing, remove this cup from me: nevertheless not my will, but thine, be done" (Luke 22:42). And so it has been through the centuries, through the days of the apostolic church, down through the years of persecution and struggle to our present day. Among the many stories in my collection on the power of prayer, I have selected for this book several from different parts of the world.

I had heard Haggai 2:8 and Psalm 50:10 all my life, as the Bible was read daily in our home, but God's claim to ownership of all the silver, the gold, and the cattle on a thousand hills did not have much special meaning to me. Then, in my teens, I heard about George Mueller, that man of faith, who housed and fed hundreds of orphans in England without ever asking a penny of anyone.

Now I have read of many times during the spreading of the message of the second coming of our Savior, when God supplied needed funding of gospel work in a similar way, sometimes testing the faith of the workers until the last moment. Some of those faith-building stories have found their way into this collection.

The Lord still heals in our day. "If thou wilt diligently hearken to the voice of the Lord thy God, and wilt do that which is right in his sight, and wilt give ear to his commandments, and keep all his statutes, I will put none of these diseases upon thee, which I have brought upon the Egyptians: for I am the Lord that healeth thee" (Exod. 15:26).

This promise was given by God to His chosen people. He led them through the wilderness, showing them the way by the cloud during the day and the pillar of fire at night. He fed them with manna, and gave them beneficial laws to promote and maintain their health. Furthermore, the Lord was going to intervene in a very special way at times to reveal his mighty power to heal. The stories on this subject are evidence of His healing power in our day.

Through my busy years of teaching, I noticed that stories of God's direct intervention in the lives of His servants began to appear more and more frequently. I kept on filing them away, and my folders became thicker and thicker. It seemed evident that the battle between Christ and Satan is getting more intense as the end draws near. In 2 Peter 3:10, God promises that this world will be burned up and that there will be a new heaven and a new earth, free of sin and pollution. Anyone old enough to remember the last few decades can see the changes and recognize that this old world is drawing rapidly to an end. "Even so come, Lord Jesus!"

When I retired I found the time to put this anthology of stories together. I have told them here just as they were told to me so long ago. I send it forth to encourage those who believe in and prepare for the second coming of the Lord.

Mabel Tupper

Acknowledgements

I would like to express appreciation to the many friends and relatives who have helped me with this book. Special thanks go to my daughter-in-law, Irene Tupper, and her twin daughters, Laura and Lisa, for many hours spent typing and re-typing the manuscript. Laura also spent many additional hours in very careful, painstaking work with Mr. Tobler in perfecting the manuscript.

I am also grateful for permission to reprint stories from the following Seventh-day Adventist publishers, organizations or individuals:

Pacific Press Publishing Association, Nampa, Idaho, for stories that are taken from the book *In the Land of the Incas* by Fernando Stahl, from the periodical *These Times* (now merged with *Signs of the Times*, formerly a publication of the now-defunct Southern Publishing Association), and *Our Little Friend*.

The Review and Herald Publishing Association, Hagerstown, Maryland, for stories that are taken from the book *The Hand That Intervenes* by W. A. Spicer, from the periodicals *Guide*, *Youth's Instructor*, *The Advent Review and Sabbath Herald* (or the *Adventist Review*, *The Review and Herald*).

The Quiet Hour, broadcasters and telecasters, for stories taken from *Quiet Hour Echoes*.

Marilyn Joyce Applegate for the story "Kidnapped in the Desert."

Len Barnard for the article "Three Dreams in New Guinea."

Martha Duffie for the story "Healed from Bubonic Plague."

Mary Weiss Futcher for the story "My Would-Be Attacker."

Dr. Minon Hamm for the story "The Angel on the Andes Trail."

Chester Westphal for the story "Saved By an Army in Columbia" from the book *Heretic at Large* by Wilma Ross Westphal.

The compiler has made great efforts to contact every single one of the authors (or their families or other owners of the copyright) whose stories appear in this publication, but it was impossible to locate them all. A considerable number of them have died. For several, no address could be found, so they could not be reached. Their stories are included here with the conviction that the authors would welcome their republication and that they would be happy to see their stories given further circulation in order to be a blessing to yet a larger reading public.

If there should be any subsequent editions of this publication, the compiler would be most happy to correct any inadvertent errors or omissions and to include more specific acknowledgements that go beyond the information given in the opening statements preceding each of the stories.

A Special Thanks

Just after he finished the polishing touches on the manuscript of *Angels At Pincher Creek*, the editor, Gustaf Tobler was called out of retirement by the Seventh-day Adventist denomination to Switzerland to begin a thrust for religious literature in the German Language. Mr. Tobler, a German-born Swiss, attended schools in Switzerland and Germany, as well as in England. He is an expert on German history and language, and was Editor in a German Publishing House in Hamburg before World War II. He worked in the German Language Department as Book Editor for Pacific Press Publishing Association until his retirement when PPPA moved from Mountain View, California to Idaho a short time ago.

Mr. Tobler was very exacting in his work, and every minute detail was checked, and letters of permission gained to republish articles. He was even aware of language changes in the stories from Africa and this affected his editorial work. As for the stories compiled for this book, Mr. Tobler would not permit inclusion of any story that was not clear in the facts beyond a shadow of a doubt. If there was any question as to accuracy or validity, the story was omitted at his insistence.

I feel that Mr. Tobler was called by inspiration of the Lord to be a leader in the German works to provide religious literature in the truly remarkable times of change, after the fall of the Berlin Wall in 1989. The Seventh-day Adventist church is fortunate to have had such a man available to bring the gospel through the written word at such a time as this. It was a real privilege to work with Mr. Tobler in the publication of this book.

Contents

Chapter 1   Angels at Pincher Creek 12

Chapter 2   Unexpected Rescue . . . . . . ' 15

Chapter 3   Trapped in the Desert 18

Chapter 4   Where Are the Watchmen? 21

Chapter 5   The Angel in the Mine 25

Chapter 6   Angels Rescue the Stahls 29

Chapter 7   The Angel on the Andes Trail 34

Chapter 8   Saved by an Angel Army in Colombia 38

Chapter 9   The Fourth Man in the Boat 42

Chapter 10   My Would-Be Attacker 44

Chapter 11   An Angel Filled the Wood Box 47

Chapter 12   A Lighted Path in Dark Woods in Sweden 49

Chapter 13   As Bright as Noonday 51

Chapter 14   The Gospel Given to Mt. Roraima Indians 54

Chapter 15   The Bushman's Story 59

Chapter 16   Papuan Aborigines Walk Into Sabbath School 67

Chapter 17   When the Sun Topped the Mango Trees 69

Chapter 18	Three Dreams in New Guinea	72
Chapter 19	The Voice in the Swamp	77
Chapter 20	"Stay and Canvass"	79
Chapter 21	Kata Rangoso	85
Chapter 22	Answer at 3:25	90
Chapter 23	The Prayer and Faith of Inani	93
Chapter 24	Manna Fell in Africa in 1939	96
Chapter 25	God Was Ready the Day the Banks Closed	99
Chapter 26	Remarkable Answer to Prayer	106
Chapter 27	From the Heart	106
Chapter 28	A Miraculous Healing in Malaysia	108
Chapter 29	Through Death's Door	114
Chapter 30	Healed From Bubonic Plague	117
Chapter 31	Called on God	122
Chapter 32	The Healing of Nondis	124

Chapter 1
Angels at Pincher Creek

The first story to move my heart so powerfully was told to me in Calgary, Alberta, Canada, in the early winter of 1926. Attending a colporteur convention for the first time, it was my good fortune to room with a dear, experienced, elderly woman colporteur. In the evening, when it was time to sleep, we talked about the events of the day. "Let me tell you what happened to me just before I left Pincher Creek to come to Calgary," my roommate began. And thus was born the story, "Angels at Pincher Creek."

My husband and I canvassed together in the little town of Pincher Creek, trying to knock on every door. We finished the town together. There was only one road through the town. We separated, each taking a part of the road. We intended to take both sides of the road and go as far as the scattered houses lasted.

As the houses on my stretch of the road began to thin out, some people warned me with words like these: "Don't go to the last house on the road. There is a real mean woman there. She screams and swears at anyone who comes there. Her brother is just as bad. We all just simply leave them alone."

When the house came into view; more details were added. One person said, "They have a big, fierce dog that attacks anyone who comes into the yard. There is a big stump in the backyard where he stays, and he is never tied up. Those people are really crazy. No one goes there."

Soon all other houses were behind me, and I walked on. There was that last house sitting all by itself on that lonely road. I was a little frightened, and I began praying in my mind: "Lord, I know that a colporteur must go to every home. I know you can protect me from harm. Be with me, Lord Jesus." So I walked on with courage.

As I came close, I could see that the snow was drifted against the front door of the house. I knew the front door was sealed up against the cold winter winds. The only trail led around to the back door. I could see the corner of that big stump at the back. I knew that near the stump lay that fierce, untied dog, ready to grab hold of any visitors.

Just at the last moment, I lost heart and hurried straight down the road, over the hump, down the hill, and out of sight of the house. By the road was a big rock, swept clear of snow by the wind. I sat on it to rest and think for a moment.

Kneeling on the rock, I asked the Lord to forgive me for losing my courage. I asked Him again to give me protection, and then I walked back up the hill. At the gate again, I opened it without hesitation and walked the trail around the corner of the house to the back. There was that big, fierce dog lying quietly by that large stump, apparently asleep. He raised his head, looked at me briefly, laid his head down again between his paws and closed his eyes as before.

When I knocked on the back door, the woman opened it immediately. She must have been standing there waiting. She said, "How did you get past the dog?"

I told her the dog seemed asleep.

Then the woman said quickly, "What do you want?"

I pulled out my prospectus and began telling her immediately about the book I was selling. Her brother stepped up beside her and they both listened quietly for a few moments.

At length, the brother said, "I don't think we are at all interested, but I want to ask you a question. What did you do with those two men that were with you? Did you have them hide behind the corner of the house?"

I was so taken by surprise that I did not know what to say or what to think. I finally said, "I do not have anyone with me, I am alone."

Then they both spoke up at once, in turn or out of turn, interrupting or just adding thoughts. "You can't tell us that. We were watching you through our front window as you came down the hill. There was a man on each side of you. They were with you as you first came down the road, past the gate and down over the hump out of sight. And they were with you when you came back up the hill and through the gate. They were with you as you disappeared around the corner of the house. Now where are they? Are they hiding around the corner of the house?"

I was so puzzled. All I could say was, "No, truly, I am alone." Then they closed the door. I went past the sleeping dog, out the gate and started back up the road toward town, still just as puzzled as ever. Finally it came to me. The Lord must have allowed them to see the angels who were always with me. I did not need to see them, for I knew they were there.

With a quick glance over her shoulder, the young colporteur noticed three rough looking men following her down the alley. Suddenly a tall young man appeared. "You're a colporteur, aren't you?" he asked.

Chapter 2
Unexpected Rescue

This next story happened in the latter days of World War II when everyone had to use ration books. It was inconvenient to have soap and some foods rationed, but the rationing of gas and tires was a serious problem for those who really needed to travel.

Colporteurs visited our church in Placerville, California, one Sabbath morning. Their leader invited a young woman who had recently come from Los Angeles to speak. I was touched by her dedication. Instinctively I felt that this was a person who was wholly dedicated to the Lord.

Another meeting was announced for the afternoon, and we were determined to hear more. We arrived early, so I had an opportunity to visit with the young woman from Los Angeles. Just before we parted, I said, "Let me tell you a story that a woman in Canada told me." I then told her the story of the angels at Pincher Creek. My listener's eyes got big, and she said, "I must tell you something that happened to me just last week."

"I was getting ready to come to the meetings in Placerville, but three of my tires needed replacing, and my spare was poor. I went to the Ration Board and asked for permission to get four new tires. They told me it was impossible to get new tires until the old ones were completely gone. They said I could get a new tire at Bakersfield or Fresno, so I drove slowly and carefully in that direction.

"Suddenly I had a blowout. The rain was pouring down steadily, so I sat in the car until a lull came in the storm. I put on my raincoat, took off the ruined tire, and put on the spare. Then I drove on through the storm. Soon there was another blowout, and I knew that the spare was done for. Again, I sat in the car while the rain poured down.

"After a while a police officer stopped. Coming up to my window he asked me what the trouble was. Indeed, he could see the flat tire. I told him that it was the spare. The police officer said that I was very close to Fresno. He assured me that if I drove slowly and carefully, I could make it without damage to the rim. He also told me where the Ration Board would meet at seven o'clock that very night. I followed his directions and soon arrived in Fresno.

"I found the street before seven, and parked my car by the entrance to the alley.

Then I simply sat and waited. Soon I saw three big, rough-looking men sauntering down the street. They eyed me in the car, glanced at each other, said a few words, and waited expectantly. I noticed it at the time, but thought little of it.

"Glancing at my watch, I noticed that it was time for me to go to the meeting. I got out, locked the car, and began walking quickly down the alley toward the place where I'd been told the Ration Board was to meet. It was getting dark now, and to my horror, I heard footsteps behind me. With a quick glance over my shoulder, I realized those three big men were following me. I was terrified at first, but I figured that if I could just reach the place of the meeting, I would be safe. Upon arriving at the appointed place, I was puzzled. The place was dark and the door was locked. I turned now, and glanced at the three men. They had stopped, too, and stood watching me.

"Now I really was frightened. But suddenly a tall young man appeared at my side. I didn't see where he came from. He was simply there. He looked down at me and spoke the only words I would have answered to a stranger, 'You're a colporteur, aren't you?'

"I was surprised and puzzled. I replied, 'Yes, but how did you know?'

"Flashing me a quick smile, the tall man said, 'Don't you remember that Pastor Jones asked me to go with you when you were ready to come here?'

"I reflected for a few seconds and replied, 'No, I don't remember that.'

"The three big men saw me talking to this stranger and moved on down the alley. They were soon out of sight.

"My new friend said to me, 'Now just what is your problem here?'

"I poured out my story of the tires, and how I had been told that the Ration Board would meet this evening at seven o'clock. I said that I came at the appointed time, but that the place was obviously deserted. I was alone here in a strange town and felt at a loss as to what I should do.

"'Come along,' my companion said. 'Let's walk to the drugstore across the street and see if they can give us some information about this.'

"At the drugstore, we were told that this was, indeed, the night of the Ration Board meeting, but that the time had been changed from 7:00 to 8:00. I was assured that if I went to the meeting, the Board would take care of all my tire needs.

"Back out on the street, I remembered something else I had wanted to ask at the drugstore. I turned to my friend and said, 'Oh, there is one more item I want to ask about! Just wait here, and I will be right back.' I dashed in for just a moment and came right back out again, but my new acquaintance was gone! I looked up and down the street, running from corner to corner, but he had disappeared as mysteriously as he had appeared."

When the story was finished, I said, "Before you left Los Angeles, the pastor prayed for you. Did he ask the Lord to send His angel with you as you started your work?"

"I have thought and thought," the young woman replied, "but really I cannot remember the pastor asking for an angel to accompany me. The leaders usually do ask that before we go out, so I suppose he did."

Chapter 3
Trapped in the Desert

First told by Marilyn Joyce Applegate in the *Adventist Review*, August 1, 1985.

"Are they not all ministering spirits, sent forth to minister for them who shall be heirs of salvation?" (Heb. 1:14)

In the pre-dawn dark, Vernon Grout hoisted a five-gallon water can into the back of his Datsun pickup. He had to be prepared in case his radiator acted up. Once behind the wheel, he left his home in Victorville, California and headed northeast on I-15. There was nothing to indicate that today would be anything more than a routine trip to Nellis Air Force Base, near Las Vegas for the 8:00 a.m. mechanic's troubleshooting class Vernon was teaching. "Don't get up, Ruth," he told his wife. "I'll eat breakfast on the way."

The August sun already felt hot as Vernon left the restaurant in Baker and turned onto the freeway. The monotonous grade to Halloran Summit was all too familiar. It was the halfway point between home and his destination. Cacti, sagebrush, and Joshua trees dotted the parched alkaline desert, and buzzards soared lazily overhead. Sidewinders wriggled into the sand under rocks to avoid the shriveling Mojave sun.

Vernon had almost reached the summit when he saw a gray Buick with its hood up. Steam poured out of the radiator. Remembering the water can in the back, Vernon pulled to a stop near the off ramp for Halloran Springs, got out, and asked, "Need some water?"

"No, I have water," came the gruff reply from a young man working under the car.

Vernon turned to leave, only to come face to face with a tall blond man who appeared behind him. "We could use a push," the second man said.

Vernon nodded and climbed into his truck, thinking that the blond man must have been in the bushes beside the road. He wondered what to make of this ordinary-looking, but strange-acting pair with very short haircuts.

"Wait there a minute." The taller man raised his hand toward Vernon and jerked his head for his partner to follow him behind the Buick. After lifting the trunk lid the two strangers talked in low tones for some time.

Vernon, anxious to be on his way, kept his eye on the rearview mirror. Finally they stepped around and motioned for him to pull his Datsun in behind them.

"I'll push you to the service station at the top of the off ramp," Vernon said. There was no response, so he repeated himself. The two men got in their car, and Vernon began to push.

At the station entrance the Buick turned sharply, blocking his exit. The men waved to be pushed across the freeway overpass. Thinking they intended to turn back to Baker, Vernon continued to push. Then the men yelled back at him, "Push us out into the desert."

Almost immediately the road narrowed and turned to dirt. Soft sandy banks fell sharply away on each side, leaving no room to turn around. The air felt stifling and dry. Occasionally Vernon saw the two men glance back. He thought they seemed nervous.

Suddenly Vernon became aware of someone sitting beside him in the cab of his pickup. It was a dignified, well-dressed man in a gray business suit.

"Push them as fast as you can," the new passenger urged. "In a quarter of a mile you will come to a turnaround. Turn quickly and get out of here, for they intend to kill you."

Startled, Vernon leaned forward and tightened his grip on the steering wheel, straining to see the road ahead. He couldn't help glancing sideways at his passenger, but the man was gone! Vernon was sweating now, jaw clenched, breathing hard. He shoved his foot down on the accelerator and forced himself to concentrate on the speedometer. The men in the Buick had the car out of gear. They were clearly not trying to get it to start. Vernon fought to gain enough momentum to push them clear for his turn.

Just as the man in the gray suit had said, there appeared a dirt circle made by heavy road-building equipment. If he hadn't been told beforehand, Vernon would have seen it too late. His foot hit the brake, but to his horror, the bumpers locked! Panic seized him. "Lord," he cried, "don't desert me now!"

With racing heart, Vernon released the brake and braked hard again. The bumpers went down. He lifted his foot, and the bumpers unlocked. Now the Buick was braking, trying to block him. With only a little clearance, Vernon spun his pickup around. The two men leaped from the Buick, cursing and waving their fists. Swirling dirt obscured them as the pickup sped away.

Vernon taught his class of aspiring mechanics that morning, not daring to let his close brush with death impact his emotions until the job was done. Then, as he thought back over all that had happened, he began to tremble. The newspaper often featured mysterious disappearances; he might have been one of them.

Some time later, when his emotions had settled, Vernon and his wife drove to the dirt road. At the point where the man with the gray suit had warned him, he checked the odometer. It was exactly one quarter of a mile to the turnaround.

Chapter 4
Where Are the Watchmen?

VonAsselt was a Christian Missions pioneer in the East Indies. In 1856 he worked in the wilds of Sumatra. The missionary and his wife were conscious of the dangers that threatened them from fierce headhunting tribesmen. Night after night, that they maintained their courage by claiming the promises of God.

After two years, VonAsselt and his wife moved to a quieter place. One day a visitor came from the region where they had first pitched their camp. The visiting chief hesitated a long time before making his request. Finally he began:

"Now *Tuan* (Teacher), I have yet one request."

"What is it that you want?" the missionary prompted.

"I would like to have a closer look at your watchmen," said the chief.

Puzzled, the missionary said, "What watchmen do you mean? I do not have any."

"I mean the watchmen whom you station around your house at night, to protect you," the chief insisted.

"But I have no watchmen," VonAsselt said again. "I have only a little herdboy and a little cook, and they would make poor watchmen."

The man looked at the missionary incredulously, as if he wished to say: "Do not try to make me believe otherwise, for I know better." Then he had a fine idea: "May I look through your house to see if they are hidden there?"

"Yes, certainly," the missionary said, laughing. "Look through it; you will not find anybody."

So the chief went in and searched in every corner, even through the beds. He came back very disappointed.

Then VonAsselt began to do a little probing himself. He asked the chief to tell him the circumstances under which he saw the watchmen of which he spoke.

The chief told how, again and again during the first days of the station, he and his men went out by night to burn the mission and to kill the missionaries. But they found watchmen on guard. They themselves felt they could not overcome the watchmen, so they hired a professional assassin to do the deed. The assassin boasted no fear of any watchmen. He went right out to do the deed, but he came back running. He said he found watchmen standing shoulder to shoulder, with weapons that "shine like fire!"

"But tell me, *Tuan*," said the disappointed chief, "who are those watchmen? Have you never seen them?"

"No, I have never seen them."

"Did your wife not see them?"

"No, my wife did not see them."

Then "*Tuan*" went in and brought a Bible from his house. Holding it up, he said, "See here; this book is the word of our Great God, in which He promises to guard and protect us. We firmly believe that word; therefore, we do not need to see the watchmen. But you do not believe; therefore, the Great God has to show you the watchmen, in order that you may learn to believe."

As Amos lowered himself down the mine shaft on the new rope, it began spinning him around, faster and faster. His hands were sweaty, his head was dizzy, and he could see nothing at all. Suddenly his hands slipped. "Oh God, save me!" he cried.

Chapter 5
The Angel in the Mine

In the late 1890s a young man, Amos Hash, experienced a sudden deliverance from imminent death in a mine. His story, as told to Frances Shafer, appeared in the January 15, 1963, *Guide*.

In the year 1897 my brother and I bought a piece of land in the lead country of Missouri. We wanted to mine lead and zinc.

Already a one-hundred-foot shaft had been sunk straight down through the rock, and a drift had been dug back into the earth at the fifty-foot level. A drift is a tunnel leading off the main mine shaft. It was to this drift that I made my way on the never-to-be-forgotten day when I went down on the new rope.

I swung on the rope in the shaft, letting my hands slide until they should come to the knot, where I wanted to get off. As I went lower, the full force of my weight pulled on the new rope, and the rope began to unwind slowly. New rope has many twists in it before it is well stretched. I didn't think of this fact that day, but the weight of my body was serving as a very good stretcher.

By the time I came near the knot, the rope was whirling me about faster and faster. I held on tightly, hoping it would stop its turning, but it pulled tighter and tighter, and whirled faster and faster, and soon I was dizzy. I was down just fifty feet, and fifty feet farther down was solid rock.

Faster and faster I turned. My hands gripped tighter. They were getting sweaty and my head was spinning and I could see nothing. That little knot was the only thing between me and the hard-rock bottom. I could not see the drift opening at all, and I was powerless to save myself. My breath was gone. My stomach was sick. My muscles cried for rest. Then my hands slipped.

"Oh, God," I cried, "save me!"

A hand reached out and drew me firmly by the shoulder into the open drift. When my feet touched the solid rock, I limply dropped that churned rope. A kind voice said, "You are sick, aren't you?" and a hand led me to the wall, where I sat down upon the hard floor.

I lifted my eyes to my deliverer. He was someone I had never seen before. He was a young man, dressed in dark trousers and a clean white shirt. I lowered my head, for I was weak and still dizzy, and then I raised my eyes to thank my new friend.

He was gone!

There were two ways to reach that spot. One was the way I had come, and I knew he had not come that way. The other was through a narrow drift from another mine, some two hundred yards away. It was a very narrow, dirty tunnel. No clean white shirt could have come through there unspotted.

A thrill went through me as I realized that God had answered my call for help by sending an angel to deliver me. No one could ever convince me differently. That was sixty-five years ago, and this one experience has been a source of strength and faith to me through all those years of my life. Don't ever neglect to call upon the Lord. He will hear you, as He heard me.

The priests began to turn the Indians against the missionaries. When Fernando tried to save the five horses, he was struck on the head with a stone. Meanwhile, an attempt was made to torch the thatched roof of the hut where the missionaries lived. The Stahls prayed earnestly that God would save them.

Chapter 6
Angels Rescue the Stahls

Anna Carlson Stahl (1870–1968) was born in Sweden, and Ferdinand Anthony Stahl (1874–1950), of German descent, was born in Michigan. Anna and Ferdinand met in America and were married in 1892. In 1902 they became members of the Seventh-day Adventist Church. They decided to take up medical training, attending Madison College and then Battle Creek Sanitarium to take nursing. Upon completion of their training, they opened a successful treatment center, first in Cleveland, Ohio, then in Akron, Ohio.

In 1909 the Stahls offered themselves for foreign mission work. They would pay their own expenses for the trip. They were sent to work among the Aymara and Quenuani Indians in Bolivia. After two years, they were also assigned to work with the Peruvian Indians. They established a permanent mission station at Plateria, Peru, where he built a school, a church, and other buildings.

After the Stahls made a short visit to America, interest was aroused in their work, and three young couples came to help them at Plateria.

Fernando and Ana (as they were called in Spanish) decided to visit some of the outlying areas that had been on their minds for some time. They were invited to visit the village of Quenuani. They spent some time helping the sick and planning for an establishment of a school in that village.

Elder Stahl told of the rescue by an angel army in his book, *In the Land of the Incas*, published by Pacific Press Publishing Association in 1919. Currently reprinted by TEACH Services, Inc.

We were much impressed with the advantages at Quenuani for reaching thousands of Indians. It had boat connections with Bolivia and with Puno, our railway station to the coast; and there was a large market located at Yunguyo, only three miles away, where the Indians of Bolivia came in great numbers to do trading. The Indians pleaded most earnestly that a missionary be sent to them, and they wanted a school also. We promised to send them help as soon as we had anyone to send.

We lectured among them, and treated the many sick people they brought to us. One day we heard rumors from the town nearby that the priests were telling the people to kill us. The Indians about us seemed to be quite nervous over the matter, and told us there was great danger that the priests would raise a mob against us. We reminded our friends that we now had religious freedom in Peru, so we did not think that harm would come to us, much less that we would be killed. We did not realize the viciousness and ignorance of the priests, nor to what extremes they would go. We continued there for nearly a week.

One morning we saw a great crowd of people coming toward us, away out in the valley. As they came nearer, we saw that two priests were leading the mob. Many of the people were on horseback, and some were armed with rifles and shotguns. As they came nearer, we recognized among the crowd men of authority from the nearby towns. We could not believe that harm was meant for us. Near us was a building where the priests usually held their religious feasts, and we thought they were coming to celebrate some such service.

We noticed Indians coming from all directions, until there were fully 500 gathered together. The priests talked to them for two hours, and gave them alcohol to drink, then led them within one block of the hut where we were staying. Here they addressed the mob again, and we afterward learned that they were inciting the people to kill us, telling them it would be an honor and that they would not be punished.

After talking to the people for about an hour, the priests set off what is called the *fugata*, a sort of large skyrocket, which is a signal in these savage sections for attack at a bullfight, or anything of that sort. We were surprised to see that insane mob led by the lieutenant governor, the authority that should have protected us! He was mounted on a large horse, and was calling to the people to surround our house.

We thought even then that they were only trying to frighten us, but on they came, gathering large stones as they approached. Many were armed with long, steel-tipped whips and clubs. The first thing they did was to cut loose our five horses, and stab them with knives, so that they stampeded down a ten-foot bank, and galloped wildly off across the valley. I tried to stop the horses, but was stoned by some of the mob. One stone wounded me severely on the head, and the blood blinded me. I almost fell, but Mrs. Stahl pulled me into the hut and closed the door, just in time to avoid another terrible volley of missiles.

In another moment, however, hundreds of stones crashed through the door, smashing it into bits. The yard was filled with shouting, frantic Indians. We quickly piled our baggage in front of the opening in the door to prevent them from forcing their way in. They were shouting loudly in the Indian language, "*Pichim Catum!*" which means, "Catch them and burn them!" They tried to push the baggage aside, and kept striking at us with their steeltipped whips. The very fact that so many were trying to force their way in at one time, slowed them down a little. Above the yelling of the Indians, we could hear the laughter of the priests.

In all this time, we had not forgotten to seek the Lord. We were ready to meet death for Him if He so willed. I hastily wrote a few lines to our coworkers and children at the home station, asking them to go on with the work. Mrs. Stahl prayed with the two Indian women who were with us in the hut. Our three native young men were brave and true, and were only concerned for us. With great difficulty I restrained Luciano from rushing out upon the mob. Had he done so, he would have been torn to pieces in a moment.

At this juncture, the priests called loudly to the Indians to set fire to the straw roof; and soon some were coming with torches to obey the command. One of them climbed up on a pile of stones to light the roof; but as he applied the torch, the Indian woman who owned the hut jumped up on the stones beside him, knocking him off: and pulled out the burning straw with her hands. Just as she succeeded in tearing out the last of it, she fell down, and some of the straw fell on her bare head, burning her severely. She afterward proved to be a very important witness because of this.

Other Indians were preparing their torches to set fire to the hut, and we had given up all hope of rescue. Suddenly, the whole mob, priests and all, withdrew. We came out of the hut in time to see the priests mounting their horses quickly, and fleeing across the valley, the mob following them.

We asked a frightened-looking Indian who stood nearby why these people had fled so suddenly. He said, "Don't you see that great company of armed Indians coming to defend you?"

I did not see them. I turned to Mrs. Stahl, and asked her if she did. She said, "No." The Indian insisted that there was a great army of Indians coming to help us. We looked around, but could see no one. God sent His angels in the form of armed Indians to rescue us. There is no other way to account for what occurred.

I was feeling very weak from the loss of blood, so I rested on the floor of the hut to regain my strength. Just at dusk, an Indian woman came, bringing our horses. She had followed them for six miles, running "in the strength that the Lord gave," as she herself expressed it. We quickly saddled our horses, and under cover of a fierce storm rode away from the place.

We suffered intensely from cold, and our clothing was wet through, but we rode on and on. The lightning sometimes blinded us, and at other times it flashed to show us the way. We heard that the people in the next town had also been incited by the priests to rise up against us, so our Indian brethren led us by a road that did not pass near this place.

After riding about fourteen miles, Mrs. Stahl told me she was cold and weak, and feared she would fall from her horse. She was not able to go on. We had eaten scarcely anything that day, so we stopped right there on the side of the mountain, spread our wet blankets on the snow, and tried to sleep for the rest of the night. At daylight, we gathered up our frozen blankets, and continued our journey to the next large town. We arrived in Juli about noon.

The authorities there had already been informed of the attack, and were distraught over the incident. They promised to bring the guilty parties to justice. We did not push the matter because we believed that God permitted only that which would work together for good. One of the largest mission stations we have is now flourishing near the place where we were attacked.

The following translation shows how this incident was regarded by many, even among the Catholics in the area. The article was published in the *Puno El Siglo* of June 21, 1916:

CONCERNING THE CRIMES IN ONE OF THE VILLAGES OF THE PROVINCE OF CHUCUITO

> The scandalous events that have just happened in one of the villages of the Yunguyo district profoundly exasperate the mind of every sensible person. The priests, Don Julio Tomas Bravo and Don Fermin Manrique, on the fifth of the present month, go to Quenuani, together with twelve citizens, heading a great multitude of Indians; they celebrate mass in the chapel; they preach to the ignorant multitude the extermination of the unfaithful; they frighten them into setting out to victimize Mr. Fernando Stahl and his wife, who are engaged in establishing a school for the native children, in the house of Clemente Condori. The mob break into the house, they attempt to burn it, they throw stones, they howl, they break the head of the Protestant missionary, who miraculously escapes with his life; with knives they hack and cut their horses, making flight impossible. Meanwhile, the Catholic priests, those sainted (!) men with the instinct of Nero, rejoice over their work, laugh and celebrate the mortifying and criminal scene.
>
> Such is the savage act, which, to the shame of the province of Chucuito and of the republic, has been committed by those who style themselves representatives of that benignant apostle and martyr of humanity called Jesus Christ.

Without any doubt, there will be none, however strong an apostolic and Roman Catholic he may be, who will fail to denounce and condemn the brutal outrages that have been committed, after the celebration of a mass in which justices of the peace, lieutenant governors, and other notables, implored the Most High to kill, rob, and burn the human devils, and this in the twentieth century and in the full light of day.

Chapter 7
The Angel on the Andes Trail

Harold Clinton Brown may have been the first Adventist student missionary. He went to Colombia as a colporteur in 1917. Isaiah 52:7 was Harold's inspiration: "How beautiful upon the mountains are the feet of him that bringeth good tidings, that publisheth peace; that bringeth good tidings of good, that publisheth salvation; that saith unto Zion, Thy God reigneth!"

Harold wanted to bring the good news of the Savior's soon return to people who had never heard it. He found these people in the mountains of Colombia. At the close of his junior year of college, Harold took two years to do colporteur work before returning to finish college and get married. Harold and his wife served together in Latin America for a number of years. Not wanting to take any glory to himself, Harold never published his experiences in the mission field, aside from a brief, two-column piece, which appeared in *The Review and Herald* in 1919.

In 1964 upon his return to the United States, Harold related his experiences to a family friend, Mrs. Minon Hamm. To her we owe the preservation of this faith-building story, which was first published in *Guide* on July 31, 1974, under the title, "Go with God" by Dr. Minon A Hamm. It is abridged here.

Harold Brown, just twenty-one years old, was traveling by horseback over the great central range of the Columbian Andes with a young Colombian companion. Harold was perplexed. He had felt so sure that he was following the guiding hand of God in coming to Colombia as a colporteur. But things were not going as well as he had expected. Now he and his companion were all alone on this hot dusty trail. They were not even sure that they would be able to get over the summit to the nearest town by nightfall. Harold knew that the high altitude would make the air very cold after the sun went down.

Harold was feeling low, but he could not tell that to his companion, Tulio. He already felt that his friend was getting discouraged too.

More than a week ago, Harold and Tulio set out with fifteen books, and twelve were still left in their saddlebags. They had sold only three books in more than a week.

At the tavern that afternoon, Harold and Tulio had met some intimidating mountain men. One of those half drunken men had threatened them, to the amusement of the others. Harold hoped that they would not meet any of those men again. And yet, there was among those ruffians one young man who had listened intently to Howard's description of the books. Wistfully, the lad said, "I wish I could read."

And that was the problem: so few of the people could read. Why should he try to sell books to people who could not read?

Harold looked ahead up the trail. Was that another mountain man standing there by his horse as though waiting for the boys to catch up with him? As they approached the man spoke: "*Buenas Tardes, Senores!*" (Good evening, gentlemen!)

Right away Harold noticed that this stranger was different from the other men they had met. To begin with, in the midst of this dusty wasteland the man was dressed in immaculate white. His open, friendly face reflected confidence and integrity.

"*Para donde van, jovenes?*" (Where are you headed, young men?) The voice was pleasantly refined.

"We're trying to reach the village just over the mountain before sundown. Do you think we can make it?" Harold, Tulio, and the horses were tired.

"It is far, but you will arrive in time." The stranger spoke gravely, and with assurance. He eyed Harold's saddlebags, "What brings you young men to this remote area?" he questioned politely.

"We're selling books that tell the story of our Savior's life, and His soon return." Then Harold heard himself continuing in a most uncolporteur-like way. "Almost no one seems interested in our books. I have just decided that we should give up the work." Now why had he said that? He hadn't admitted it to Tulio, and maybe not to himself. And now to a stranger?

The handsome man smiled at the boys. "*Amigos* (friends), you must not do that. More families than you think are waiting for the news that you bring. God will guide you to them and give you success." He tipped his hat and waved the boys along.

Harold fell into deep thought as he jogged on. How could this strange man's words affect him so powerfully? Somehow he felt a hope of success begin to grow again in his heart.

Now they rounded a rocky outcropping and started down a steep trail along a tumbling stream. The water was hip high at its deepest. Soon the way was blocked.

They rode down the steep bank to ford this stream as they had forded several others that day. Suddenly Tulio's horse, which was leading, stumbled. Before the boy could jump clear, both animal and rider pitched headlong into the water. They did not get up.

Harold leaped from his horse and raced to his companion's aid. Tulio's horse lay just as she had fallen, neck doubled under her, head submerged in knee-deep water. Harold thought she must be dead. And Tulio—who knew his fate? The lad was pinned underneath the horse. Harold had to get him out quickly or he would drown, if he hadn't already died of a broken his neck in the fall.

Harold grasped the horse's tail and tried to roll her off the pinned boy. The heavy beast didn't budge. Struggle as he might, he could not move the huge bulk a single inch. Pushing and pulling in agony of fear, Harold did not notice the approach of a white-clad stranger until he heard a voice from the bank behind him.

"Voy a ayudarte, amigo!" (I will help you, friend!) the man called as he swung down from his horse. Without stopping to roll up his immaculate trousers, he stepped into the stream. He grasped the horse's tail with one hand. The animal seemed to float off the boy. Then he pulled Tulio to his feet.

The youth was conscious, but seemed to be in great pain. "Oh, my leg!" he gasped. "I can't stand up!" He crumpled weakly against his helper. The stranger calmly passed his hand along the injured leg, then stepped back with a smile.

"What happened?" Tulio exclaimed. "The pain is gone! I'm all right!" He stood as strong as before the fall, looking incredulously from Harold to the stranger.

"Yes, you're all right. But you'll need your horse." The man stepped over to the animal, who still lay quiet, with her head jackknifed against her chest under the water. He touched her flank lightly. A shudder ran through her. Then she heaved, snorted, and rose up. She stood quietly before Tulio, switching her tail.

The boys searched for words to thank the stranger, but with a gesture of authority he signaled them on their way. "You have far to go, and much to do. The hour is late. *Vaya con Dios* (Go with God). He will bless your work."

Shaking their heads in amazement, the boys adjusted their saddles and climbed back on their horses. They crossed the stream, and as they climbed the far bank, they turned to wave at the stranger who had remained at the streamside, watering his horse.

There was no horse, and no man could be seen anywhere! From that moment on, Harold Brown could never doubt that God had a treasure in Columbia—people to be found and prepared for the second coming of Jesus. Nor could he doubt that scores of others would follow him in publishing the glad tidings of peace across these mountains and valleys.

Today there are more messengers carrying the three angels' messages in Colombia's mountains, plains, and cities than ever before. They walk the trails, ride mules, drive Jeeps, or ride on crowded buses. They pole dugout canoes, pilot speedboats, or fly planes. And with such a beginning, can anyone ever doubt that they "Go with God"?

Chapter 8
Saved by an Angel Army in Colombia

During the 1920s the monthly *Sabbath School Worker* sometimes carried interesting articles by E. Max Trummer. This author was the pioneer missionary to Colombia for three decades. In the early 1970s Wilma Ross Westphal spent some time with the Trummers, gathering material for several of their stories that she included in her book, *Heretic at Large*, published by the Review and Herald Publishing Association in 1976. That excellent book is out of print, but I have chosen one story from its pages to share here.

The time came when the Trummer children were old enough to leave the mission field and go back to the States to complete their education. Mail time became especially important to Max and Noema, who looked forward to the children's letters with a great deal of anticipation.

With the children gone from home, Noema busied herself with Bible studies and mission work during her husband's absences. Sometimes she accompanied him on his journeys.

On one occasion, Pastor Trummer traveled alone by muleback, making his rounds of the groups of newly interested people among the mountains and valleys of South Santander. He entered the picturesque area of the Chicamocha River where he planned to visit the village of Chicacuta. Near the village, among the well-tended farms of the Camacho family, Bible truths were changing hearts. The people were delighted to receive Pastor Trummer and study with him.

News of the conversion of the influential Camacho family to Pastor Trummer's new faith had the zealots of the village in a veritable frenzy. These leaders recognized that some great spiritual awakening was soon to take place in their area.

The local spiritual leader presided over Chicacuta and environs along the Chicamocha River. He talked to Antonio Moreno, a prominent citizen of Chicacuta, and convinced the man that he should send three well-known criminals to assassinate the "Adventist heretic" as he came over the rocky ledges of the mountains above their village.

Antonio Moreno soon rounded up the criminals and gave them firearms, knives, machetes, and other instruments of violence. He told them of the fiendish plan, promising them a goodly sum of money for their services. "Don't return until you've done away with this heretic, Trummer!" he finished.

"But we must know exactly the day and the hour that this heretic will be passing over the mountains, along the trail near yonder boulders and ledges," the hirelings said.

"Our spies will find out the exact time to expect him, and we shall let you know immediately," Moreno assured them.

Receiving this promise, the villains said, "Rest assured that this will be the last time Heretic Trummer will pass through our village. The people he has been deceiving with his unorthodox teachings will be duly rescued from the synagogue of Satan. The body of this troublemaker will be cast down into the troubled waters of the Chicamocha River upon his death."

"That's very fine idea," Moreno agreed. "Let the waters of the Chicamocha forever hide your deed of violence. May the leaders of this village reward you with many indulgences, and may the God of heaven pay you well for this brave and noble deed." Thus saying, Antonio Moreno watched them withdraw.

Before the three criminals left the village, they were notified by Moreno that Trummer was due to pass the designated spot at a certain hour that very afternoon. The men ascended the mountain forthwith, hiding among the rocks and brush near the pathway. They waited about three miles from the village of Chicacuta, near the top of a ledge that perched a sheer thousand feet above the river. Here they watched for their unwitting victim to pass.

Finally Trummer and his mule were spotted, coming up over the hill. To the satisfaction of the watchers, he was alone. They were confident that their efforts would soon be crowned with success. Trummer disappeared briefly into a narrow ravine, and they waited with baited breath behind the boulders, ready to spring upon him as he passed.

"But—what is this that has happened?" asked one criminal of another. They stood petrified with fear, for when Trummer emerged from the hollow, he was accompanied by a group of soldiers!

"Where could these soldiers have been hiding?" they asked one another in consternation. "That small ravine couldn't have hidden so many soldiers! What shall we do? They'll soon be upon us! The pathway is very narrow at this point. We can't escape in any direction! The tables have turned, and we ourselves are the victims of our own scheming!"

The would-be murderers had found a small place wide enough to crouch behind some large boulders, but there was a sheer drop-off of one thousand feet to the river on one side. On the other side the cliffs rose to a great height. They could neither turn back nor rush ahead. The pathway was very narrow for some distance. They feared that the soldiers would shoot them if they tried to escape.

As Pastor Trummer and the soldiers advanced upon them, the three outlaws stood frozen to the spot. The "heretic" nodded to the outlaws with his characteristic smile, and extended his hand amiably to each one. They couldn't keep from trembling, and their breath came in short gasps as they reluctantly extended clammy hands to him as he passed close to each one.

When Trummer and the soldiers were out of sight, one of the criminals asked wonderingly, "How did he ever get hold of a battalion of soldiers?"

"Why," marveled another, "they had to come all the way from Bucaramanga in order to protect him! How did he suspect that his life would be in danger at this particular place? We didn't even know it until today!"

"Well, there's no use to stay here any longer. We've failed in our purpose, but at least he didn't use his soldiers to shoot us down. We can thank the good saints for that," said another.

As soon as they felt it was safe, the three outlaws followed Trummer, well out of sight of their intended victim. When they finally reached the village of Chicacuta they reluctantly informed Antonio Moreno of their failure.

"But you promised to do away with that heretic!" Antonio stormed.

"Yes, but he was protected by a whole battalion of armed soldiers—soldiers of the government, no less! What else could we do but allow them to pass?"

"Wha-what happened to them? Where did they go?" Moreno demanded. "We don't know, but they were still with him the last we saw of him."

"If this is true," Antonio bellowed, "our own lives may well be in danger. We'd better lay low for awhile and let the unfortunate incident be forgotten. I-I never realized he carried that much influence with the government!"

Later, as Pastor Trummer visited with the Camacho family, he related how he had met the three men on the ledge above the river. "I glimpsed those men up there on the path trying to keep out of sight behind a pile of boulders, and I felt that they were up to no good. When I went down a little draw, I got off my mule and went behind a large boulder for a few moments to pray. I asked God to send my angel to protect me from the men who were waiting along the trail to do me harm. And you know," he went on wonderingly, "those three men, though unsmiling, just stood there and let me pass! I shook hands with them, but I sensed that they were nervous about something."

Several days later the villagers themselves told why the outlaws were nervous and afraid. Since this incident, Antonio Moreno had warned the assassins not to do Trummer any harm at this time, since he had the protection of a battalion of armed soldiers. This word was passed along through the grapevine. Only then did Trummer realize that God had answered his prayers for protection by sending, not only his own guardian angel, but a whole battalion of heavenly beings in the form of earthly soldiers. He thanked God for this manifestation of His protecting power.

Chapter 9
The Fourth Man in the Boat

A Seventh-day Adventist missionary in Venezuela, L. J. Borrowdale, told this story of angel help in time of danger. It appeared in the *True Education Fourth Grade Reader*, published in 1931.

In Venezuela, a country in the northern part of South America, one of our missionaries passed up a river in a mission boat. His assistant, and a boy to help take care of the boat, was with him. When they came to a fork in the river, they did not know which way to go. They decided to try the right hand branch of the river.

Soon they found they could go no farther. They returned to the fork and took the left branch. They passed up this branch until it began to grow dark, then they cast anchor, and went to sleep.

The next morning the missionaries continued their journey up the river until they reached a town where they were to hold meetings. After the meetings were over, they returned to the fork of the river. This time they stopped at a house and were given permission to stay the night. The missionary and his assistant went up to the house leaving the boy to look after the boat.

"Where is your companion?" the owner asked.

"He is at the boat, but he will soon be up," the missionary answered, thinking that the man was speaking of the boy.

"But where is the other one?"

"There are only three of us."

"I saw four men in the boat when you went up," the man insisted. "Your helper here was at the front, steering the boat. You were at one side, leaning over to watch; and the boy was on the other side, taking the depth of the river."

"Where was the fourth man?" the missionary asked.

"He was standing right by your side, and dressed in white."

Then the man described how the two helpers were dressed. The missionary knew by this that his host had observed carefully and correctly. The man then told the missionary that this part of the river was very dangerous.

With gratitude, the missionary thanked God that he had been saved from dangers that he knew not of. God fulfilled His promise, "The angel of the Lord encampeth round about them that fear Him and delivereth them" (Ps. 34:7).

Chapter 10
My Would-Be Attacker

Mary Weiss Futcher grew up as a foster child, shifted from one Jewish home to another. Some were good, many were difficult. Finally she became a Christian.

In the joy of being born again into the Kingdom of God, Mary gave herself unreservedly to the work of winning others to Christ. Because of her Jewish background, Mary had special success in persuading other Jewish young people to follow Christ.

At the time of this story, Mary had just begun her work as a Bible Instructor for the Manhattan, New York, Seventh-day Adventist Center. Her story was published many years after it happened in *Guide* on July 19, 1986. Her life was one of quiet consecration to the Lord, illustrating the verse in 2 Chronicles 16:9: "The eyes of the Lord run to and fro throughout the whole earth to shew Himself strong in the behalf of them whose heart is perfect toward Him."

I was so happy, I walked down the street on air. As a young Bible worker in training for the New York City Manhattan Church, I was having a thrilling day. Several teenagers with whom I'd been studying had made the choice to give their lives to Christ. I had one more call to make, but I wasn't tired. I was full of joy as I went to the next home.

I didn't expect it to take long, but it was after ten o'clock before I left. Again there were wings of joy on my feet. Both parents and the teens in that lovely Jewish home had promised to be at church the next Sabbath.

My mind replayed the last visit as I walked to the nearest subway station and boarded a train without considering that it stopped a whole six blocks away from my apartment. If I had walked another block I could have taken a train that would have taken me within a block of home, but I didn't realize my mistake until I stepped off the subway. No matter. I looked around and decided that the night was beautiful and a six-block walk wouldn't hurt me at all.

I left the subway in Harlem, and the streets were poorly lighted. But I had a song in my heart, and I headed toward home with my thoughts still on the joy of being a Bible worker. I thanked God for blessing my efforts that day and for being such a wonderful Savior. Bible verses were singing through my mind when a huge hand grabbed me from the back and yanked me into a dark, narrow passageway between two tall buildings.

My mind raced, and it seemed that time stood still. I felt myself go hot, then cold. My hands were wet and clammy, my mouth dry. I wondered wildly what the man planned to do to me. Would he rob me? Would he kill me? I knew that people had been killed for a few cents! I didn't have any money. My shoulder bag held only a Bible, several tracts, and a few other useful items, including my house key. I felt numbness ripple through me from the top of my head to the bottom of my feet, and realized with a new terror that I couldn't make a sound.

"Oh, God, save me!" I cried silently. In that instant the man dropped me as he would a sack of potatoes, and ran out screaming, right into the grasp of a police officer.

It took me a few seconds to come to my senses, but at last I got up, shook the dust off my hands and clothes, picked up my shoulder bag, and went out to the dimly-lit sidewalk where the police officer was talking to the attacker.

"Are you all right?" the police officer asked me, deep concern in his voice.

I nodded. "Yes, yes, I'm fine now."

"Do you want to press charges?"

My heart still pounded in my throat, and I hardly knew what to answer. The attacker, held tightly by the officer, begged to be released. He was hardly coherent, and kept saying that the lightning that had struck him right before he dropped me must have been from outer space.

The three of us talked a few minutes, and I explained my work and why I happened to be on the streets alone. Opening my bag, I took out the tracts and found myself giving them to the attacker. The police officer made the man promise that he would never do such a thing again, while I stood by, amazed at the turn the conversation was taking.

The police officer seemed satisfied that it was all right to let the attacker go, but first he asked us to pause for prayer. As he prayed, the police officer mentioned my name and that of my mugger. At the time, I was so upset, I didn't give it another thought.

When the man walked away, the cop turned to me. "Would you like for me to walk you home?" he asked kindly.

"Yes, please." I was still scared, and I never thought to wonder how the police officer knew my address. As we walked, he talked to me about the dangers of being in such a neighborhood at that hour of the night.

"God gave you a brain, and you must use it wisely," he said seriously. "You must think things out." He kept on talking as we walked. He spoke kindly but seriously, and with such tender love that I hugged every word to myself and have always remembered his advice.

The police officer impressed upon me the dangers of being presumptuous, of assuming that prayer would get me out of problems that I'd gotten myself into because I didn't use my head. At last we reached the lighted area of Broadway.

"Do you need to get back on duty?" I asked, thinking that my rescuer had gone far off his assigned beat.

He shook his head. "I want to see you to your apartment door."

We walked slowly. I told my new friend about the people I'd met that day, of the teens who'd given their lives to Jesus, of the family who'd promised to come to church. He listened carefully, obviously interested in my work and happy with me at the way God had blessed.

As I reached my apartment, my steps slowed. I saw the doorman open the outer door, nodded to him, then turned to thank the police officer for walking me home.

He wasn't there! Puzzled, I turned to the doorman. "Did you see where the police officer went?"

The man frowned down at me. "Police officer? I didn't see anyone, miss. You came to the door alone."

As soon as I closed my apartment door, I fell down on my knees and thanked God for His wonderful deliverance. I could hardly sleep that night, thinking … wondering. It didn't seem possible that I could have actually walked and talked with an angel!

The next morning I phoned the police station in my precinct, and in the Harlem precinct, asking the name of the officer who had been on street duty the night before. Officers at both stations told me that only patrol cars had been in the area the night before. So again, with great awe, I thanked Jesus for sending His angel to protect me.

Psalm 34:7 has been my assurance ever since that night so many years ago.

That verse says: "The angel of the Lord encampeth round about them that fear him, and delivereth them."

Chapter 11
An Angel Filled the Wood Box

We will tell this beautiful true story in a condensed form, based on an article that appeared in *The Review and Herald* of December 22, 1955. After carefully checking the details of this story, A. L. Zumwalt, then president of the Alaska Mission, and several others in the Adventist community there, were firmly persuaded of the truthfulness of this modern miracle.

A widow, Louise Dubay, lived alone in Anchorage, Alaska. Her home was heated by a wood-burning cook stove. At the time of this experience she was sick in bed and so badly crippled that she could scarcely walk. She depended on friends to bring a fresh supply of wood each day, but on this particular morning no friends came to help her. She realized that unless someone brought more wood soon, the fire would go out, and she would freeze to death. The temperature was thirty degrees below zero that February day. Mrs. Dubay began to pray earnestly for help.

Finally, as no one appeared, the last of her wood was burned. The fire went out and the room grew cold. Mrs. Dubay now prayed a different prayer. It was a prayer of resignation, telling the Lord that if it was His will, she was willing to die. Just then the door of the cottage opened, and a tall young man walked into the room carrying an armload of wood. He carefully placed the wood in the woodbin, and began to remake the fire. He also filled a kettle of water, and placed it on the stove to heat. He then went outside and soon returned with another armload of wood.

While performing this service, he kept his face to one side, so Mrs. Dubay could not see him distinctly.

Mrs. Dubay wanted to ask her benefactor whether he was an angel, but she was reluctant to do this. Finally, she asked the question inaudibly, and the young man turned toward her, smiled, and nodded his head.

"His face was so noble that I knew he was not of this world," says Mrs. Dubay.

"He opened the door, and left me without saying one word."

Was this young man really an angel? We let Mrs. Dubay give you her conclusion: "For a time I sat there like one turned to stone. Finally I thought: If he is an angel sent from God, there will not be any footprints in the snow outside the door. I forced myself to hobble to the door, opened it, and looked out on the unruffled snow in my yard. There were no footprints in the snow.

"Then I forced myself to lean against the side of the door casing, and looked around to my right, to see whether the snow had been disturbed over or around, my little pile of wood. The snow was perfectly smooth and rounded over, just as it always is after a snowstorm.

"As I closed the door to the little cabin, I knew that God did love me, and that in my extremity He had sent one of His holy angels to my assistance."

Chapter 12
A Lighted Path in Dark Woods in Sweden

W. A. Spicer was a much-loved president of the General Conference of Seventh-day Adventists for many years. Soon after World War II, he sent a short article to *The Review and Herald* telling of a strange incident, which happened to a young colporteur in Sweden. Several years later, in the January 17, 1952, issue of *The Review and Herald,* he mentioned this incident again, adding more details, along with several other angel stories from the world field. Related here is a summary of the two stories.

A young woman was working as a colporteur in the northern mining area of Sweden. She had selected one of the villages near the mines for her dwelling place, and traveled to her daily work on her bicycle. The day appointed for delivering her books proved to be one filled with delays and frustration. It was late when she finally turned her bicycle towards her home.

The road branched off the main road, taking her through a dense growth of timber, which at night was like entering a dark tunnel. She had been warned repeatedly to arrive at this point while there was still enough light filtering through the trees to guide her to the other side. Recently, some unfortunate incidents had occurred along this dark road.

Now, despite her best efforts to reach the fork in the road before dark, she found herself at the entrance of the gloomy tunnel, with not a speck of light to guide her. She had dismounted from her bicycle, then knelt beside it, and prayed a simple prayer, asking God to take care of her as she passed through the dark woods. She later said, "I knew the good Lord would take care of me, but truly I did not expect anything unusual."

She moved forward into the dark tunnel of branches. Suddenly there was light shining all around her. She looked for the source of the light, and could see light in the boughs of the trees overhead. As she continued along, the light overhead moved right along with her, staying with her until she emerged on the other side of the woods and into the welcome lights of the village. All the way through the light-filled woods, she praised the Lord, thanking Him for watching over her.

   Although several years had passed by the time she told this experience to W. A. Spicer, she was still filled with awe and reverence over this moving experience. It brought joy to her heart that the Savior had shown His love for her in her special time of need.

Chapter 13
As Bright as Noonday

This story was published in the May 13, 1952, edition of *The Youth's Instructor* by Mrs. J. W. Dortch, who experienced it with her family about thirty-five years previously when Texas was opening up for farmers and settlers.

About the turn of the century, Adventist believers established for their young people an academy in Keene, Texas, which they called the "Industrial Academy." This school grew steadily, and in 1916 it opened its doors as a junior college under the name "Southwestern Junior College." From then until now, this college (now renamed "Southwestern Adventist University") has been training missionaries to go and spread the gospel around the world.

Some years ago our family moved to Texas and bought a farm on what was then known as the western prairie. With us was our married son who lived in another house on the same farm. In September of the second year, after the wheat was harvested and most of the crops were gathered, our son felt impressed that he should go to school. He came in one day and asked me what I thought about his entering Southwestern Junior College that fall at Keene. He wanted to better prepare himself to work in God's cause. I told him that I was agreeable, but that he should talk with his father.

"Son," his father said upon hearing the plan, "that is just what I would like for you to do, and I will stand behind you."

Our boy began at once to make preparations to move to Keene. When the time came for him and his wife to go, we got up early on a Thursday morning and loaded all their belongings on two wagons. My husband and I both went along, so I could drive one of the teams back. We planned to return Friday evening in time to do the milking.

We reached Keene about the middle of the afternoon, in time to unload and get the family settled. The next morning we rose early and started home, so we would arrive before the Sabbath. We had not gone far when it began to rain. We hoped it would not rain long, but it kept right on raining a little harder all the time.

My wagon had a cover on it, but the other one did not, so we decided that my husband would hitch his horses to the back of my wagon and get in with me, in order to be out of the rain. It kept raining, and we kept going. The roads got very muddy and sticky. At times it seemed that the horses could hardly pull us through.

We reached Fort Worth at four o'clock. We had driven thirty-five miles but still had fifteen to go before we were home. Our daughter met us and visited with us for a few minutes. Then, because it was still raining, she suggested that we hasten, or night would overtake us.

When we were about three miles out of the city the rain stopped. My husband then got out of my wagon, took his team, and drove in front of me, thinking that this would encourage my horses to keep up. But the horses were so tired they stopped every few minutes to rest.

Everybody who has traveled over the west Texas prairies before the roads were graveled knows how hard it was to drive a wagon over them in rainy weather. The black, sticky mud would fill the wheels solid from rim to axle. It was slow, but we kept going the best we could.

Night came on. The clouds hung dark and low. We had no lights of any kind, and the houses were miles apart. It was so dark that one could not see his hand in front of him. We did not know where we were going, and our teams were so tired they stopped to rest often. Finally my husband came back to my wagon and said, "Do you think I had better hitch my team in front of yours and see if both teams can take us home?"

I replied, "I have heard people say that if you give a horse the reins, he will take you home."

My husband got into my wagon, and we talked things over. We had tried to bring our children up in the way of the Lord. We had kept before them the thought that Jesus is soon coming. We told them that, if time should last until they were grown, we wanted them to give their lives in helping to carry God's last message to the world. We felt that the Lord was pleased for us to take our last child to fit himself for better service. So at this point we claimed the promise of the Lord that He would never leave us or forsake us; then we started, believing that He would take us home.

The night was very dark, but we traveled on. We had not gone far when all at once it became as bright as noonday in front of the wagon. I could see the road and the horses' feet, and when I looked out from under the cover to see whether it was the moon shining, everything behind and around the wagon was as black as darkness could make it. I sat back in my seat again, and everything before me was as bright as noonday.

Just then my husband, who was driving on some little distance ahead, called to me and said, "Do you see anything?"

"I certainly do."

He called back, "Everything in front of me is as bright as noonday! Why, Mamma, the angels are lighting the way home!"

At this time we must have been four or five miles from home, but we drove on, I with my light and he with his. Every little bit I could hear him say, "Praise the Lord," and my own heart gave back the echo.

Our lights stayed with us until we reached home. When my husband drove up in front of the gate and stopped his team, his light went out; and when I drove up just behind him and stopped my team, my light went out. We unhitched our teams, put them in, and fed them. When we got into the house it was just twelve o'clock. We then had a praise meeting until two o'clock. This was a good Sabbath day for us, because we knew as never before that "the angel of the Lord encampeth round about them that fear him, and delivereth them" (Ps. 34:7). To God be all the praise!

Chapter 14
The Gospel Given to Mt. Roraima Indians

Mt. Roraima is the point where three countries, Venezuela, Brazil and Guyana, meet. About the year 1900, an old Indian chief of the Guyana slope of Mt. Roraima was visited by a shining being, as he called it. This being revealed to the surprised chief strange things he had never heard of before. He was told of the creation of the world, of the entrance of sin into the world and the fall of man. Then came the story of the promised Redeemer, His birth, life, death and resurrection. Christ's second coming in all His glory and the final end of sin was also shown to him.

The old chief was instructed to teach his people all these things, and also to teach them to observe the seventh-day Sabbath. He was taught how to lead a clean, healthful life. Next he was told that in time a man would come with a black book, and would teach them more.

Like Paul, the old chief was "obedient to the heavenly vision." He gathered his people together and faithfully taught them all he had learned. When he died, his son, who became next chief, carefully continued in his father's footsteps, teaching the tribe all the things his father had been taught.

When the missionary O. E Davis discovered the isolated Indian tribe of Mt. Roraima in 1910, he sent his story to America where it thrilled the hearts of all believers.

The next year church members learned about Davis' second visit. They heard that he had died of blackwater fever on the trip, and was buried at Mt. Roraima, The members were grieved and shocked.

From that time on, the natives at Mt. Roraima were called the Davis Indians. For fourteen years the question was put to the church: "How long must the 'Davis Indians' at Mt. Roraima wait for us to answer their call for a missionary to teach them? There was great rejoicing in America as well as at Mt. Roraima when the call was answered in 1925.

Many stories have been written about Mt. Roraima, and the original visions of the old Indian chief. In the preparation of the following story, great care has been taken to go back to original sources, searching through the records in the Heritage Room of Loma Linda University and all the accounts that have appeared in *The Review and Herald* beginning with 1911 and as late as the 1984 report of the dedication of the new church.

The Lord chose the man to carry the "black book" to the people of Mt. Roraima. His name was Ovid Elbert Davis. He was born in 1869. After completing his training in Berrien Springs, Michigan, he answered a call to take the message to a group of Indians in Alaska. His work was not received well in Alaska and his enemies threatened to tie him to a stake out on the tidelands, and leave him to drown in the incoming tide.

Davis managed to elude his would-be captors, and walked from Alaska to northern British Columbia's Fort Simpson. There he was welcomed by the Fort Simpson Indians. He spent four years there teaching them the gospel story. After he found a native leader capable of continuing his work, he returned to the United States where he was eventually ordained as a minister in Berrien Springs, Michigan, about 1905. In 1906 he was sent to Guyana.

Elder Davis made Georgetown his headquarters. There he preached the gospel to the Indians, teaching them about the time of the end and how Christ would make a glorious return to earth to take away the sin and suffering from this world. He urged them to keep the seventh-day Sabbath that was given to man at the creation of the world.

Word came to Elder Davis by the grapevine that there was a tribe of Indians on the slopes of Mt. Roraima whose people already believed the things he was teaching. They were even keeping the seventh-day Sabbath. The persistent rumors gave him a burning desire to find this tribe of Indians.

In 1910 Elder Davis made the dangerous trip through the jungles with his guide. Upon arriving at the village, he took out his Bible and began to teach the people from his "black book." This was their sign. The people rejoiced that at last the man they were looking for had arrived, and they listened eagerly.

Elder Davis stayed with them, teaching them more of the story of Jesus' love and His will for their lives. He taught them many simple gospel songs, which they sang with fervor and enthusiasm. He left them then, promising to return as soon as he could.

Elder Davis returned to "his" Indians in 1911, braving the difficult jungles. This trip was extremely hard on him, for he contracted the dreaded "blackwater fever."

He arrived very ill, and prepared for his death with two letters. He gave one to the boy with him, and the other to Jeremiah, the chief of the tribe. He left a journal containing the Christian names he had given to 187 of the people who had given their hearts to the Lord Jesus. After giving his belongings to Jeremiah, Elder Davis died at the young age of only forty-two years. The Indians lovingly buried him there on the slopes of Mt. Roraima on July 31, 1911.

Through August and September there were confusing reports about the cause of his death, but in *The Review and Heraldd* of November 2, 1911, E. C. Boyer gave the true report of the memorial service. Although Elder Davis died of Blackwater fever, it is possible that he himself did not realize the cause of his sickness. It appears that at first he thought he had been poisoned with a slow poison at a village he visited on the way. This gave rise to various rumors that were later proven false.

Jeremiah and his tribe vowed to be true to the principles of the gospel as taught by the Seventh-day Adventist church. These faithful Indians sent out a plea for a teacher to replace Elder Davis. For fourteen long years the request went unanswered. Through the years, explorers told of finding this tribe and seeing them gathered around the grave of a missionary singing songs about Jesus and his return in glory.

In 1925 a gift of $4,000 was given for work among the Davis Indians, as these people are now called. Two missionaries were sent to visit them with a promise that a new missionary would come soon and stay with them permanently.

In early 1927 Arthur Cott was assigned to this work, along with his wife, Elizabeth. Cott was able to bring with him simple healing methods to help the people, and his wife came well supplied with all the Sabbath School materials she could assemble. Her teaching was popular with both the children and adults.

In 1928 Arthur Cott wrote an article for *The Review and Herald* about their work among the Davis Indians. When they returned to America seven years later, the work was well established, and to this day these Indians are strong believers in the gospel.

Other missionaries have come and gone over the years. Recently, Lloyd Henrito, a young minister who was trained at Caribbean College in Trinidad, came to be their pastor. A church was built there, and the story of its dedication is told in the *Adventist Review*, August 2, 1984.

Fred Fernandez and three others paid a visit to these people. They flew a mission plane in, landing at the Kamarang landing strip where they were met by Lloyd Henrito with his large outboard motor canoe. Four hours later they arrived at the little settlement. They took many pictures, and stayed long enough to attend the dedication of the church.

The plane, and the motorized canoe were a vast contrast to the rough and long, tiresome, painfully slow method of travel that Davis had to use when he first made that dangerous journey through the jungles to find these Indians back in 1910 and 1911.

Now the work at Mt. Roraima is in good hands, and the church members are part of the family of believers who await the return of the Lord to take them out of this sinful world into the heavenly kingdom. How happy the old chief will be when he awakens on the resurrection morning and learns how the wonderful message he received through a shining being brought blessings to his people.

Sekuba headed alone into the unknown. Clad in his skin loincloth, he carried his kaross and a scanty supply of dried meat. He was armed only with his bow and poison-tipped arrows on this journey into the wastelands of the Kalahari desert. He went in search of the man with the "black book," as the "shining one" had commanded him in his dream.

Chapter 15
The Bushman's Story

This story from Africa was written by Gwomans Piatt Ansley and was published in the January 22, 1963, issue of *The Youth's Instructor*.

Far away in the remote, sandy wastes of the Kalahari Desert in Bechuanaland [Botswana], Southern Africa, lived the primitive Bushmen. They had never known civilization. They lived where the white man seldom goes and never stays. Sekuba was one of these little Bushmen. Though he was a full-grown man, he was barely five feet tall.

As Sekuba and others of his family group of Bushmen crept into their crude shelters one night in 1953, they had no inkling that their way of life was about to change forever. The daytime heat of the desert gave way quickly to the chill of the winter night. Near him, Sekuba kept his bow, and a quiver of poisoned arrows.

These little people among whom Sekuba slept were wise children of nature and knew her secrets. They knew the roots that yielded the deadly poison in which they dipped their arrowheads. Hidden in places they alone knew were shells of wild ostrich eggs. These they filled with water at the time of the brief rains. They knew where the watery tsama melons grew.

A wild, nomadic people who retreated as civilization advanced in generations past, the Bushmen ate raw flesh from the animals they killed, and wore the skins as loincloths. They ate snakes, rats, insects, roots—anything that would sustain life. They could find their way in the trackless Kalahari. Life's necessities they understood. They survived incredible hardships in their contest with unrelenting nature. Generations of living in this manner seemed to have well-nigh effaced the image of the Creator.

As the stars glittered in the dry, crisp sky, the night for Sekuba was suddenly brighter than day. He talked with a being who spoke from a bright fire. The next morning Sekuba tried to tell his wife and family what he had experienced. Over and over he repeated the story as their minds tried to grasp the significance of his night vision. Like all primitive peoples, they attached great significance to dreams, but who had ever heard of a dream like this! They had never seen the things he tried to tell them about.

What was the "Book" Sekuba was talking about? Considering their background, it is no wonder Sekuba's family had difficulty comprehending. Who was the "Shining One" who had spoken from the fire? Why was he so bright one could not look at him? Why must Sekuba go to the east to find the people of the "Book" and learn about God, the maker of the things of nature all around them? What was he trying to tell them about "a plan" this unseen God had for them? They could not understand the urgency Sekuba felt to go that very day in response to the angel command. "How will you speak to the people you will meet?" they challenged him as he made preparations.

He told them as he had told them before, "The 'Book' talks. The 'shining One' taught me the words of the book! I understood them and I will be able to read them."

The Bushmen speak a language of clicks and guttural sounds quite unlike languages spoken by Bantu natives. No one ever goes to the Bushmen with books. Their language has never been reduced to writing. They are fugitives who retreated before the Bantu Africans and the white Europeans.

If a rare, courageous bushman ventures anywhere near these inhabitants of civilization it is to hunt straying cattle and goats to add to the meager fare of wild game. They are often considered enemies and thieves to be hunted by both Bantu and European. They are people who shoot their poison arrows from ambush. They are a people to be feared.

Sekuba's wife and relatives made no attempt to remind him of the dangers he would find along the way. The awe and wonder of his night vision impressed them too. Together they traveled as a group, each day drawing nearer the eastern border of Bechuanaland, hunting to sustain themselves as they went.

Finally, on the fringe of civilization, they found a few scattered Bushmen who knew a little more about their Bantu neighbors. Sekuba left his family near them. His people believed him when he said he would return for them after he found the people with the "Book."

Clad in his skin loincloth, carrying his *kaross* (a blanket made of animal hide), and a scanty supply of biltong (dried meat), Sekuba set out. He was armed with his bow and poison-tipped arrows, as he advanced eastward alone into the unknown. He was going in obedience to the angel's directions.

Some 150 miles from his original starting place, and many days later, Sekuba hesitantly approached the scattered huts of some Bantu farmers on the border of one of the African reserves.

Bushmen are known more by reputation than by sight, and so the startled tribesman at the first hut was filled with fear and apprehension to see the dusty, loin-clad Sekuba. The wizened little man of the desert seemed shy and showed no signs of belligerence. The arrows were in their quiver, and the empty bow in his hand calmed the African's impulse to flee. Timidly the little Bushman waited for the African to speak.

"I see you," greeted the Bantu according to African custom.

With dignity Sekuba returned the greeting, then asked, "Where will I find the people with the 'Book'?" When the amazed Bantu tribesman found no words for a moment, Sekuba continued, "I have come to find the people who worship God."

"You speak our language!" exclaimed the African.

"The 'shining One' taught me," Sekuba stated simply, then explained more of the night vision he had seen. "Can you take me to one who can teach me more of the 'Book'?" he asked.

"This is marvelous! Yes, I can take you to our pastor. He lives near." The African entered his hut to explain to his family. They followed him outside, wide-eyed, eager to glimpse a real Bushman who said a supernatural being had taught him their language.

Together the African, tall and ebony-dark in tattered old European clothes, and the dusty little brown man in a loin skin, kaross over his shoulder, walked quickly along the path toward more scattered huts where other Africans stared in amazement at the unexpected sight of a Bushman in their midst. Their progress was delayed as Sekuba's escort briefly explained the miracle of a Bushman speaking Tswana. A few others joined them as they proceeded toward the pastor's house.

In the gathering dusk, the group arrived at the humble dwelling that had real windows with glass panes. When the pastor heard their excited story he spoke to Sekuba.

"These speak for you, but I would like you to tell me for yourself."

The pastor, clad in a black suit with a white clerical collar, brought his chair outside and sat, while his people squatted African fashion on the ground.

Sekuba, never before in the presence of civilized people, was not abashed. A feeling of joy and gratefulness for the success of his journey filled him. Gladly he gave his testimony and explained the wonderful vision that had sent him on this journey. Every African listened in silence.

At last Sekuba asked humbly, "Have I found the people who worship God and have the 'Book'?" The pastor, deeply moved, rose, entered his house, and quickly returned with a Bible in his hand. Sekuba's eyes lighted. Clapping his hands softly and bowing his head he exclaimed, "That is it! That is the 'Book'"

"This is the end of your journey," exclaimed the pastor. "You shall stay with me tonight." He led the group in prayer. Then the marveling Africans returned to their huts. The pastor made the Bushman comfortable in the little hut that served as his kitchen. His servant prepared food for him. Sekuba lay down to sleep, glad to have found the object of his search.

Then another vision was given him. The angel came again. "This is not the true church," the "Shining One" said. "You must continue your search. You must find the Sabbath-keeping church and ask for Pastor Moyo."

When morning dawned, obedient to his heavenly visitant, Sekuba explained to his host, "I must leave you. I cannot stay here. The 'shining One' came in the night and told me to find a people who keep the seventh day as Sabbath."

The pastor could not believe his ears. At last he found his voice. "This is the chiefs church. Would the chief be wrong? You have not understood." With a note of irritation in his voice he spoke to the Bushman.

Sekuba was firm, yet respectful. "Sir, I have not misunderstood. These things were shown me plainly. There are people who worship God on the seventh day. Please tell me where I may find them."

At this the pastor's voice grew loud and angry. He threatened Sekuba. Neighbors began to gather. The pastor enlisted their sympathy, and anger mounted against the little Bushman. When he had a chance to speak, he never wavered from his story, always saying, "The 'shining One' bids me find the seventh-day church."

That an unkempt Bushman in skins should presume to question the pastor's church was unthinkable. It was, in fact, treason—heresy. The Bushman remained adamant, insisting he must find the Sabbathkeeping church. Ridicule and abuse were heaped upon Sekuba but failed to intimidate him.

Then they placed Sekuba under arrest for defying the church of the chief. A growing mob proceeded with their Bushman prisoner the remaining forty miles to Serowe, capital of the Bamangwato tribe of Bechuanaland.

Defenseless, the little Bushman was brought before the chief. In his own desert country, Sekuba would have hesitated not a moment to kill a stranger who threatened him. What must have been his thoughts as, far from familiar scenes, he stood before the chief of the unfriendly tribesmen and listened to the accusations against him? But he was true to the angel vision and answered fearlessly and courteously. He told the chief that so long as he should live he would remain true to the unseen God who gave him the message of his dream.

The Sabbath message was not exactly new in Bechuanaland. The chief himself knew personally of Adventists, for his wife was one. He now commanded Sekuba to be silent, but Sekuba refused to stop, saying that as long as he had life he would continue to speak of the wonders revealed to him.

The gathering threatened to become unruly and out of control. Not daring to allow this matter to climax in trouble, and not being able to take action himself; the chief and his court took their prisoner and went to Serowe and asked the native commissioner for judgment.

This man, a European wise to the ways of Africa, heard the story with patience. At first, he too joined in threatening dire penalties for disturbing the peace, but Sekuba remained firm. His testimony was given again for the true God and His Sabbath. The white man was amazed that a Bushman, speaking Tswana, though unlearned and alone, should thus continue to cling to his story of angel instruction. His sincerity was evident. A feeling akin to awe crept over him.

The white man weighed the evidence thoughtfully. After all, Sekuba had committed no offense. It was most remarkable, his ability to converse in fluent Tswana. His courtesy and courage demanded respect. He turned to the chief, his court, and his expectant, restless followers. Then he turned back to the humble Bushman as the crowd became silent.

The white man addressed Sekuba, "You have committed no crime. You are free to go and to speak of your faith." Then he gave an order for the crowd to disperse and return to their homes. The little Bushman was to continue his search unmolested.

Alone once again, somewhere outside Serowe, Sekuba spent the night where darkness found him. How to find Pastor Moyo—in what direction to go—he did not know. He had done his best, but his efforts had brought him into trouble that was nearly disastrous. His wisdom was insufficient for this great problem.

Twice the "Shining One" had talked to him. In simple faith, alone in the desert, he now talked to the unseen God. He prayed that He would direct him, give him a sign. Then he slept the sleep of a trusting child.

With the dawn, Sekuba saw near the distant horizon a small mist-like cloud. That, in the clear dry air of the semi-arid country bordering the Kalahari, Sekuba accepted as his sign. Patiently he set out at once to follow it. Each day it was there, a small cloud, always to the northeast and ahead of him, leading him on, for seven days and 118 miles. Along the way he carefully avoided roads and men. One mistake was enough.

Sekuba approached Tsessebe, a little settlement beside the railway that threads its way from Cape Town north across the great African continent toward the Congo. He was a small, but now inconspicuous brown man clad similarly to those living in the little village. Somewhere, perhaps in Serowe before he left the shelter of the native commissioner's court, Sekuba had acquired some European clothes.

The cloud that had gone before him disappeared. As the rays of the setting sun touched the peaceful countryside, Sekuba made preparations for the night. Would he find the pastor named Moyo in Tsessebe?

Next morning as he walked steadily toward the town, he met a Bantu African. The tribesman greeted him with some curiosity, but the small brown man clad in shabby European clothes, carrying a kaross and speaking Tswana excited no great wonder. The Bantu directed him to the village, and with no difficulty Sekuba found the pastor's house.

"Dumelong" (Good morning), greeted the Bushman visitor as the pastor answered the knock at his door. The kaross he carried had slipped, and the arrows were visible. The startled pastor studied his visitor intently and recognized that no ordinary African stood before him. He, as did other Africans, harbored some fear of Bushmen, but courtesy bade him invite the stranger in.

Sekuba once again told his story in Tswana while the pastor listened with growing awe and wonder. "I am commanded to find the people with the 'Book' who keep the seventh-day Sabbath," concluded Sekuba.

Gladly Pastor Moyo brought out his worn Bible.

"That is it. Yes," said Sekuba eagerly. "You are the people." There was joy in his face, joy in his heart, when he knew he had reached the end of his journey. But he must know more—much more.

All that day they talked. Pastor Moyo explained about the first coming of the promised Messiah as a little baby. He showed him from the "Book" why Jesus came and how He would come again.

That night it was the pastor who dreamed. Fear of the Bushmen reaches deep in those who have lived near these people. A text was shown him: Ezekiel 36:8. Awakening he rose quickly and lighted a candle. He found the text and read: " But ye, O mountains of Israel, ye shall shoot forth your branches, and yield your fruit to my people of Israel; for they are at hand to come. " Fear of the Bushmen left as peace came into his heart. God had other "branches," other people soon to come.

Sekuba stayed two weeks with Pastor Moyo. Daily they searched the Bible together and drank in the wonderful message of salvation. Before Sekuba left to return to his own people he extracted a promise from Pastor Moyo that he would come and teach them more. Sekuba planned to live in the Nata crown lands. These government lands were set aside, but not part of the reserves occupied by various Bantu tribes. Rather than return to the uncertain fortunes of nomadic Bushman life, he wanted to settle on the crown lands with those of his people who would join him in beginning a new life.

Pastor Moyo traveled by bicycle to Sekuba's new home. He stayed a week the first time, obtaining his food from an African storekeeper at the trading post. His days were spent instructing the Bushmen who came to hear. Other Bushmen making the transition into civilization lived in that area and were interested.

They had everything to learn, including the ways of civilization. Plowing and cultivating fields, they learned from more advanced neighbors among whom they settled. For the first time they learned about taxes. "You are men among your fellow men, not animals roaming the desert," the District Commissioner of Francestown told them when they came to register and pay tax.

A few months later, in 1954, Sekuba was baptized. He was the first fruit of his tribe. In 1955 his wife, brother, and sister were ready for baptism.

Pastor Daniel Mogegeh baptized these people. He says they have phenomenal memories. They retain what they are told and memorize long passages of Scripture in a short time, without forgetting. They are intelligent, and make loyal Christians.

Sekuba retained the ability to speak, read, and write the Tswana language until his death in 1957. He was ordained as a church elder, evangelist, and pastor of the first Bushman church. Before his death, ten more of his tribe were baptized. The latest report gives the number as more than forty.

When the angel visitor first appeared to Sekuba, Africa was relatively quiet. Today there are winds of every kind of thought to confuse and destroy faith. Before the need was evident, God in His mercy allowed this miracle of grace to be performed that the confidence of His people might remain firm.

African pastors and believers met and talked with Sekuba, the Bushman who obeyed the angel's command. These people provide a living testimony that God has set His seal upon His Sabbath by directing a primitive Bushman to the church that keeps it. They can know of a certainty that God Himself is leading a people out of every tribe and nation.

Since this story appeared in 1963 in *The Youth's Instructor*, the work has steadily grown among the Bushmen tribe of the Kalahari Desert. Reports with pictures of some of these people have been published in *The Review and Herald*.

At present the work is well developed among the Bushmen. There are now many true believers, and there are schools for the children and also for the adults who wish to learn to read. The Bushmen moved where gardens could be raised and no longer needed to hunt for food. These wild bushmen, of whom all Africans were afraid, will be among those who meet the Lord when He comes, and share in the everlasting kingdom.

One Sabbath morning a group of heathen natives dressed only in mud-painted bodies and a few leaves for meager covering with bone decorations through the septum of the nose walked quietly to the back of the church and did their best to imitate the worshippers in every phase of the service.

Chapter 16
Papuan Aborigines Walk Into Sabbath School

The following modern Macedonia call happened in New Guinea. It is adapted from a report, which appeared in the *Sabbath School Missions Quarterly* of May 21, 1972. The account was originally written by Donald Kelly of the Youngberg Seventh-day Adventist Hospital in Singapore.

It was Sabbath morning in a beautiful valley nestled against the foot of one of the mountains in the highlands of New Guinea. The teachers and students of the school were assembled for Sabbath School, when in walked a group of heathen natives who sat down quietly in the meeting. They had mud-painted bodies, with a few leaves for meager covering. Bone decorations poked through the septum of their noses.

Quietly, the best they could, the unusual visitors imitated the believers in every phase of the worship service. After church they told their story.

A few weeks previously, their beloved chief was very sick. It was evident that he would die soon. Just before he died, he began to speak to them in gentle, subdued tones: "I have had a dream, and in my dream I have been instructed to instruct you." He told them that in his dream he had been accompanied by a beautiful shining being along a narrow pathway, through barren wastes, through weeds and thorns, bypassing ravines until they emerged into a place where beauty surpassed all he had ever seen or imagined.

The beauty of the country, and the perfect happiness of the inhabitants, evoked within him an intense desire to stay. He expressed his desire that he and all of his tribe might be allowed to enter and remain.

The chief was told that entrance to the city was free, but all who wished to enter must first find the key to the city. His guide then instructed him as to where he might find the key. The instructions contained a description of the place where the chief would find the answers to his deepest longings after truth.

After this instruction, the chief was commanded to return to the village and relay the details to the members of his tribe. As soon as he delivered the details and received a firm assurance from the tribe that they would obey his commands, the chief lay down and quietly died.

An excitement of quiet intensity pervaded the village. What did it all mean? Never before had they witnessed such an occurrence. As soon as the funeral rites were completed, a representative group from the village set out to an unknown destination, their only guide being the information they had received from their chief. They traveled for days. When they came in sight of the Seventh-day Adventist mission, they knew that their journey was at an end. Here they would learn more about the beautiful land and the key to the city.

The travelers told the people at the mission, "This is the place where we were told we would find the way of truth and the key to the city. In obedience to the commands, we have come to seek your help. Will you help us? Will you teach our tribe the true way? We are all waiting."

Chapter 17
When the Sun Topped the Mango Trees

For many months, the believers in the village of Yekea in the unnamed African country had not been visited by a missionary. But now, suddenly, they were sure the overdue visit would take place in two days. What made them so sure? Missionary G.L. Goodwin, who was welcomed by an expectant crowd, wrote the following report published in the *Adventist Review* of October 16, 1980.

It had been a long and tiring day. With mission workers, I had visited outschools and outstations, counseled with village headmen, and prayed with and for believers who had not been able to make contact with our mission for almost a decade. Fording the rivers, following the tortuous tracks from passing Land Rovers and insurgents, all added up to what should have been a good night's sleep. But as I lay on my camp cot and looked up through the corrugated metal roof I could not sleep. The light of a full moon shone through the machine-gun-riddled roof. During a recent rebellion planes had strafed the school.

One reason I could not sleep was an earlier conversation with my African brethren: "Bwana, we must go to Yekea. We must go! There has been no missionary there for many moons. Please let us go!"

"But there is no time," I replied. "We have many things to do here before we leave. I don't see how we can take such a trip."

Several times a day during that entire week, they had come to me with that same plea. As we finished our worship on Thursday evening they made one last attempt. It was this final plea that kept ringing in my ears.

Darkness had settled down. The quietness was broken by sounds from the African bush as the night creatures began their activities. Lying on my back with my hands folded under my head, I asked, "Lord, what do You want me to do? Should we go to Yekea?"

The thought struck me as if I had been hit with a flash of lightning. We must go to Yekea! We must go! Slipping into my bush clothes, I went to the place where my brethren were sleeping and told them that we would leave at four in the morning.

Brother Uhen, the field treasurer, passed the word around quickly. It would take about fourteen hours to make the seventy-mile journey over the tortuous track. We wanted to reach our destination before Sabbath.

Leaving Talla Station in the predawn darkness, we bounced, creaked, and ground our way up hills and across grasslands, forded rivers, and arrived at Yekea just as the sun was touching the tops of the mango trees to the west of the station.

When we drove into the play area near the school building that served as our church, the place was teeming with people, almost as if an anthill had exploded. As the truck stopped, a man jumped onto the cab step, stuck his head through the open window, and counted, "One, two, three... " and then he asked, "How many people are there?"

"Nineteen altogether," I replied.

"They're here! They're here! They've come! Hurry, hurry, it's almost Sabbath and we are waiting for worship!" the man shouted.

He directed each of the nineteen passengers to certain homes that seemed already prepared to welcome guests. Brother Walter Serals and I were shown our room in the home of the head teacher. Our bath water was already in a long dugout tub. Because it was nearly Sabbath there was not time for a leisurely bath.

Baths having been hurriedly taken, clothes having been put away, we made our way to the meeting place with Bibles in hand. A man rushed up, exclaiming how happy they were that we had arrived safely. Another mentioned how wonderful it was to have missionaries visit them again after such a long time. Just before the meeting began, someone stated that they had been preparing for two days and they hoped everything would be satisfactory.

"Two days!" I exclaimed. "Brother, I didn't know I was coming until last night, after the tree hyrax began its evening song. How could you have known about it for two days?"

As the familiar Sabbath hymn "Day Is Dying in the West" was being sung reverently, we marched into the overcrowded building. In my mind was a jumble of unanswered questions. It was apparent that these people had been expecting us. Everything was well arranged. There was even a baptism scheduled for the next day. Food was prepared, places to stay arranged for, bath water drawn, and luscious fruit awaited us in our rooms.

The suspense was so great that I do not even remember what I preached about. I do remember that after the service, as we made our way out to our sleeping quarters, the head teacher finally explained the mystery.

On Wednesday night one of the dedicated teachers had a dream. In that dream he saw two missionaries and seventeen African workers and families in a large green truck. They pulled onto the school grounds just as the sun was touching the tops of the mango trees. He was told to have everything prepared so that their guests could be ready to welcome the sacred hours of the Sabbath when the last bit of the sun would sink beyond the western horizon.

This experience impressed me with God's interest in His earthly children. It also impressed me with the importance of careful preparation for and observance of the blessed Sabbath day. We always must be ready to welcome our Special Guest on Friday night, when the sun begins to touch the tops of the mango trees.

Chapter 18
Three Dreams in New Guinea

In *The Review and Herald* of August 28, 1971, Len Barnard, missionary pilot in Papua New Guinea for many years, reported the experience of a man who had three significant dreams within six days. In a letter dated October 23, 1988, and written to the compiler of this book, Barnard gave the following explanation of the fact that dreams have sometimes played an important role in the conversion of uneducated heathen to God: "Those days were stirring times. The good Lord graced them with many wonderful dreams because of their [the heathen's] illiteracy and inability to read the Good Book."

"Suppose you like find im life ino savie finish you must behind in Seven Day Mission" (If you want to obtain eternal life you must follow the Seventh-day Adventist Mission).

This startling message was spoken in Pidgin English in a series of dreams. Chief Karkar, of Maramun Valley in the New Guinea hinterland, was an influential man. The message in his dreams stirred him and his whole clan of sixty men and women to make a persistent plea for an Adventist missionary in his village. In all, this chief had three dreams within a period of six days, and these he related to me through an interpreter. Squatting beside the open fire on the floor of the grass hut where I was to spend the night, this humble man of the jungle gripped my attention as he told me the story.

"In my first dream," he said, as he thoughtfully stirred the fire with a stick, "I walked along a jungle trail until I came to a point where it was divided. One well-used branch, led along the floor of the valley to the left; the other branch, which was narrower, climbed abruptly upward. Intrigued by the challenging trail to the right, I decided to follow it.

"For several hours I plodded laboriously upward, clambering over fallen trees, wading through mud, and tripping over tangled tree roots. As evening approached, I saw, half hidden among the tall trees, a small grass shelter. It looked deserted. Stooping low, I pushed myself through the small doorway and sat on the earthen floor, happy to rest.

"Suddenly a voice spoke to me out of the darkness. Slowly and deliberately, the voice said, 'Are you satisfied with your mission and your way of life?'

"Struggling against fear, I replied, 'Yes, I am quite contented with my way of life. I attend worships and meetings fairly regularly.'

"'But,' the voice continued, 'you are still living much the same as you did before the mission came to your village. You still practice your heathen sing-sings and indulge in all the spirits that accompany them. You still believe in talking to your evil spirits when in trouble. And let me ask you, does your mission help you or your people when you are sick?'

"To this I could not reply. The words burned deeply into my mind. After a short silence the voice spoke again, 'If you want to obtain eternal life, you must follow the Seventh-day Adventist mission.'

"This suggestion troubled me because it cut across many of my private practices and ambitions. I knew of the Seventh-day Adventist mission across the valley from our village, and one day its local leader had visited our village and had spoken to us about the love of God. He had shown a picture of this great God's Son coming here with myriads of angels to take the faithful believers to His better land. I had never heard this story before, and it fascinated me. Then the missionary visitor walked over to a mother with a sick baby and after a few words of sympathy, prayed to his God, and marvelously the child was healed. This profoundly impressed us all. But we preferred our own mission, for we did not have to give up anything to belong to it.

"Once again the voice spoke, 'I want you to go back to your village and tell all your people what I have told you. Then I will visit you again to see if you have done what I asked you to do.'

"'But now,' the hidden voice said, "I want you to stand outside the hut and listen. Follow the noise you hear, but beware, for you will be challenged by guards who will try to spear you. Grab the spears and hurl them back. None will harm you."

"Going outside, I could hear the throbbing drums and the deep-throated dirge of a heathen sing-sing. Following the noise, I found a clearing in the bush, where I came upon a scene of typical heathen licentious dancing. It was a writhing mass of humanity. Men were beating drums and singing mournful tribute to the spirits of their evil gods. Behind this scene was a church. As I proceeded toward it, some men approached me, hurling their spears at me. These I was able to grab without being harmed and to throw back at my attackers, who finally fled.

"As I peered through the doorway into the dimly lighted church, I saw the natives coming from their sing-sing and carnal pleasures. They bowed down before the leader of the church to confess their wrongs so as to be forgiven. Then they went outside to indulge in the same evils again. In amazement I stood there for some time until I realized this was reminiscent of happenings in my own village. Then my dream faded away.

"Awakening from my sleep and feeling deeply disturbed by my dream, I sat pondering beside the fire in my hut until the reluctant dawn crawled over the eastern mountains. I decided to call the villagers together and tell them my dreams. At this stage I was not prepared to dismiss my present native missionary, whom I had invited to my village more than a year ago. Furthermore, I was quite happy with my present way of life. But this dream had jolted me and raised serious doubts in my mind.

"Calling the villagers together, I told them a portion of my dream. I also told them I believe this dream meant I was going to die soon. A hushed silence followed this announcement.

"In a dream two nights later, I was walking down the same mountain trail. After several hours of toiling, I entered the same little hut I had entered in my former dream. After some time, I heard the now-familiar voice speak to me. Displeased with my actions, the voice said in a chiding tone, 'I am ashamed of you.'

"With a start, I woke from my dream feeling justly rebuked. Around my neck hung a token of my former 'Christian' mission. This I tore off and flung away, now determined to be true to the divine directive.

"Even before dawn began to scatter the morning mists below my village on the ridge, I summoned my people to gather before me. This time I told them in greater detail my first dream, omitting none of it. Then I recited my latest dream. My people rejoiced as I told them I was not going to die. They listened intently when I informed them the mysterious voice was telling us to follow the 'seven Day' mission across the valley if we wanted eternal life in the better land.

"Soon the whole village was astir. We decided where to locate a new mission that would follow the same teachings as the 7-day mission. Since the whole village was now enthusiastic about the change, I selected a central site. Some of the men were sent to outposts for materials for the missionary's hut while I led a delegation to visit the 'seven day' missionary. He willingly accompanied us back to our village.

"This was not the last dream," Chief Karkar continued after a pause. "Four days later I followed the same trail in my dream, going much higher, past the little hut and up to the mountain. Finally, I met a lone man beside the pathway who was very friendly and spoke to me. When I asked him what he was doing, he said he had come up the mountain to prepare a dwelling for his villagers, who would shortly be coming to feast on the valued karuka nuts." (This practice is common in the New Guinea Highlands. These oily nuts grow on the pandanus palm at an altitude of eight to ten thousand feet, and are considered a delicacy. Every year some tribes still fight savagely to defend their ancestral rights to their nut-bearing palms in the moss-covered jungle.)

"My newly found friend told me to continue walking up the mountain and I would see what he had built. This I did and was amazed to find a gigantic building on the mountaintop. Its roof reached out of sight and from the inside a bright light emanated. Venturing forward to look inside, I saw men and women with lighted faces of joy, reverently bowing before a great central column, which was the source of light.

"Cautiously entering, I saw a huge banquet room stretching as far as I could see to the right. Angels in white robes were hurrying back and forth with armloads of karuka nuts and fruits of all kinds. Overcome by curiosity, I asked one of the angels what they were doing. He told me they were preparing for the big banquet. While looking at the loaded table, I was told I could attend the banquet if I fulfilled the requirements. This aroused my keen interest.

"Early the next morning, I summoned the clan to assemble. This time they were eager to know whether I had had another dream and a new message. Among them was Warai, the missionary who accompanied me back to the village when I visited the nearby Adventist mission.

"After I related to my people the dream that was puzzling me, Warai stood up and told us all the true meaning of the dream. He said that Jesus, the Son of God, died on earth to save us, and then returned to heaven. There He is preparing homes for us and is soon coming to take us to heaven, where we will attend a big feast with all the faithful Christians from all lands. Jesus invites all of us to this great banquet, and now we are to get ready.

"My people became excited, and some of them began to build their huts near the new mission site. They renounced their heathenism immediately."

Needless to say, I was spellbound, listening to this astonishing narration by Chief Karkar. How gracious indeed of our Lord to stoop down to this lonely valley hemmed in by mountains soaring 13,000 feet high and accessible only over a 10,000-foot pass. This whole Maramun tribe is but 2,000 or 3,000 strong, being sparsely scattered throughout the valley. This is surely one of the "uttermost" parts now hearing the gospel. The Maramun Valley church membership is growing rapidly. Its nearly 500 Sabbath School members throughout the rugged valley are in seven separate companies. Every quarter, I conduct a baptism, and the church will soon have another hundred members.

Last year I flew into the valley to hold a baptism on "Baptism Sabbath." My missionary, Sarp, said he had chosen a more open site by the stream since a larger crowd than usual would be witnessing the ceremony. Then he told me that a native missionary of another organization had dreamed an impressive dream.

In the dream, the missionary saw a plane. Two men disembarked. One of them conducted a baptism by immersion, which he had never seen in reality. When he heard that I was flying over in a few days to baptize some new believers he told Sarp he would like to attend, and also bring his flock. This he did and he is now preparing for baptism by immersion himself Again, how amazing!

Chapter 19
The Voice in the Swamp

This strange story from New Guinea was found in the *Sabbath School Missions Quarterly* (Fourth Quarter 1985). It was to be told in connection with supplementary notes that were available. The additional material is incorporated in the following account.

Leo Jambby was born into a large family in the coastal region of Irian Jaya, the western half of the Island of New Guinea. His parents had desired to have a girl, and could not see how they could raise another boy. Leo's aunt took him at the age of two and kept him until he had to return home to attend school.

Leo first attended a mission school, and played hooky continually until his aunt threatened that she would buy him no more clothes unless he attended regularly. When he started studying in earnest, he learned to like school and was an excellent student. He did so well in the school that he was sent on to one of the leading high schools and finished second highest in the nation.

It was discovered that Leo had a drawing talent. When he entered a national contest, he got the second prize. Next he entered college and graduated with an engineering degree. Then he began teaching drawing at the same college.

About this time, the Dutch left Irian Jaya, and the Indonesian government took over. Leo began to fight the government. Consequently he got into trouble and fled to the neighboring country of Papua New Guinea. In a skirmish with an armed patrol he was shot in the arm and fled for his life, along with his friend Peter.

Leo's left arm was twisted, broken and bleeding badly. They lost their way and ended up at a swamp. Evening came and Leo said: "I'm not going any farther. In the morning if you meet with any of my friends, come back and find my body." The two men found a raised piece of ground where Leo could lie down and die.

During the night Leo dreamed of his childhood. His parents were teaching him the Lord's prayer. He recited it with them and sang, "What a Friend We Have in Jesus" in Malay before lapsing into unconsciousness.

Some time later Leo heard a voice speaking. "You are dying," it said. "You've been fighting the government. But now you are lifeless. If you have life tomorrow, remember that the life you get is not yours. It will be borrowed."

"I will give you life tomorrow" the voice went on, but I want you to do something for me. Don't fight for any government. I want you to fight for my coming kingdom. Get ready. It is coming soon."

The voice then told Leo how to get out of the swamp, and how to reach the government patrol station. He was given the name of the officer who would help him, too. "You will be in the hospital at Wewak by six o'clock tomorrow evening," the voice concluded.

"And where do I go after that?" Leo asked, his curiosity aroused.

"Don't ask that question," he was told. "Wherever you stay, that's the place I want you to be."

Peter was surprised to come back and find Leo alive and ready to continue at sunrise. They followed the path Leo had been shown, and everything turned out as had been promised. He was indeed in the Wewak hospital by six o'clock.

Because Leo spoke neither English nor Pidgin English, he was unable to communicate with anyone. Hearing of his predicament, Pastor Lionel Smith, an Indonesian missionary, formerly working in the Far Eastern Division, requested that he be allowed to visit Leo. Permission was refused, but Pastor Smith soon became desperately ill and was admitted to the hospital. There he met Leo and gave him a copy of the book *The Desire of Ages* to read. He also shared some magazines in the Indonesian language. This was Leo's first contact with Adventists.

"I knew this was part of the way that the man in the swamp pointed out to me," Leo says, "and I discovered the kingdom of God for which I am to fight."

After his discharge, Leo settled on Manus Island. His arm continued to bother him, so he was sent to Rabaul for further surgery. There he met Rheum Puku, a Seventh-day Adventist doctor. Dr. Puku studied with Leo, took him to church, and helped him prepare for his baptism in March 1970.

Upon his discharge from the hospital, Leo was invited to teach theology students at Sonoma College how to paint evangelistic charts. While teaching there, he studied theology, and married Elizabeth, one of the elementary school teachers.

"That experience in the swamp was the turning point in my life," said Leo. "When things get tough, I remember the vision in which I was told that I had to do this work."

Chapter 20
"Stay and Canvass"

This story was published in *Guide* on January 21, 1970. It seemed so amazing to the editors that they wrote to the author, Thelma Norman, asking her if this story was really true. Back came a letter from Abe himself. It said, "TO WHOM IT MAY CONCERN: The story... is a true account of some of my own experiences. I have given Mrs. Norman permission to write it and submit it for publication. (Signed) A. G. Ortner, July 15, 1968."

The lights blinked on in the dormitory, signaling the arrival of five o'clock in the morning. Abe sat up and pulled the quilt up around his shoulders. He had slept only fitfully all night, and the coming of morning did not please him at all.

Abe had a problem. He felt sure that the Lord wanted him to do colporteur work this summer, and he didn't want to go. He felt that he did not have enough education to sell books. He had tried it the summer before and had hoped he'd never have to do it ever again. Still the impression persisted that he was supposed to go canvassing.

Glancing over at his still-sleeping roommate, Abe thought, "If only I had Fred's education and confidence, I would not mind doing colporteur work one bit."

Then, suddenly, it seemed to Abe that his roommate and all the furniture disappeared. The door opened, and a stranger walked in. The stranger took a roll of paper from under his arm and unrolled it. Abe saw a large map. It was a most unusual map, for on it were clusters of what appeared to be bloody fingerprints. Pointing to some of them, the stranger said, "Abe, if you don't go canvassing this summer, the blood of all these people will be required of you in the judgment." Rolling up his map, the stranger walked out, and immediately the room was as it had been; the furniture was all back in place, and Abe's roommate was stirring sleepily.

"Well, Abe," Fred mumbled, still not fully awake, "How come you are awake before me this morning?" The expression on Abe's face awakened Fred quickly. "Why, Abe! What has happened?"

Abe told his roommate about the experience he had just had, and Fred answered, "Abe, that was a message from the Lord! You'd better go canvassing!"

"I know," Abe said softly. "I wouldn't dare disobey."

As soon as school was out, Abe and a companion went to their assigned territory along the Missouri River. The other man had several summers of colporteur work to his credit, so he decided how to divide the territory between the two workers. Abe found that, like the patriarch for whom he was named, he had been given the brown, burning hills away from the river while the other took the more prosperous river-bottom farms.

Day after day Abe tramped the hills, stopping faithfully at each home, but seldom making a sale. The country was in the clutches of a prolonged drought, the crops were dying in the fields, and nobody wanted to buy books.

Weeks went by, and Abe despaired of earning the scholarship that would make it possible for him to attend school the next year. Then he got a letter from his father saying that he could get work as a carpenter, building three houses, and the wages would be enough to earn his tuition for three years.

Abe thought it over. After all, if he made enough money at building to pay for three years' schooling, he could still canvass the following summers. Yes, maybe it would be better if he went home and worked. Surely the Lord didn't intend for him to stop his education.

So, Thursday noon found Abe, a suitcase in each hand, trudging down a deserted street toward a little railroad depot. Suddenly a voice, kind but firm, spoke in the drowsy noontime atmosphere.

"Abraham, where are you going?"

Abe knew that voice and where it came from, and he answered, "All right, Lord! If You want me to stay and sell books, I will. But I want to be sure, Lord, so I'm going to cast lots."

Moving his suitcases out of the center of the dusty road, Abe sat down beside them. Then he took two pieces of paper and on one he wrote, "Stay and canvass," and on the other he wrote, "Go home." Folding them he placed them in his cap and shook them. After a short prayer, he picked out a piece of paper and opened it. What would it say?

"Stay and canvass," he read.

"I'll try again," he decided. "I want to be really sure." This time he took a larger piece of paper and tore it in two. On one piece he wrote, "Lord, I'll stay and canvass all summer, even if I don't sell one book, if You'll see that I have money for school next year." On the other he wrote, "Go home and build houses."

Seven times Abe put the papers in the hat and chose one. Seven times the message came out, "Stay and canvass!"

Greatly encouraged, and with the confidence that he was doing what the Lord wanted him to do, Abe went back to canvassing. Up and down the hot, dusty hills he went, never disheartened even though he sold no more books than he had before.

A few minutes before nine o'clock one morning, Abe was going down a small country road. He had just completed one unsuccessful canvass, and the next house was already in sight when he heard the voice speak to him again. This time though, the voice whispered.

"Abe," the voice said, "go over that little hill to your right. You'll find a house there. Go and give your message!"

Abe could see the little hill, and since there was no road in the direction he had been ordered to go, he went across the field. Sure enough, when he got to the top of the hill, he could see a house down below.

Crossing the barnyard, he fumbled at the gate. He could not open it, so he went to the second gate nearby. The second gate opened easily, and he went on to knock at the door.

At once the screen door opened with such force that it seemed as if it would be torn from its hinges. Abe was startled, but he began his explanation to the woman standing there. "I'm engaged in a line of Christian work," he said, but got no further.

"Come in! Come in!" the woman interrupted eagerly. "Come right in!" Almost before he could collect his wits he found himself sitting in the parlor.

Taking out his copy of *The Great Controversy*, Abe began his canvass. He covered the first two chapters and was telling about the third when the woman interrupted him.

"Young man," she said, "before you go any further, I want to tell you something."

Abe resigned himself to hearing once again about the drought and how nobody could afford to buy books in times like these. Oh, well, anyway, he had tried!

"You see," said the woman, "some time ago my husband and I decided we wanted to do just what the Bible teaches, so we began to search for a church that followed the Bible. First to one church then to another we went, but every time there was something to disappoint us. Once we thought we had found the right church, but one day I asked the minister a question about the doctrines he preached and he told me that if we were going to question the church we needn't come back, so we didn't go there again."

Abe was listening intently, for this was certainly a far different story from what he'd expected to hear.

The woman continued. "Finally we decided to ask the Lord to send the Bible truth to us. For a whole year we've prayed." She paused and wiped her eyes. "Last night an angel came to me in a dream. He beckoned me to follow him, and pointing out a window he said, 'Look!' When I looked I saw a young man dressed in light trousers and a dark coat—just as you are dressed—coming across the pasture over the hill. He came to the barnyard gate, but he could not open it, so he went to the second gate and came through. The angel said, 'That man is bringing you the truth for which you have been praying. He will come across that hill at nine o'clock tomorrow morning.' I was so happy I woke up and sat right up in bed. My husband awakened then, and I told him my dream. He thought it was an ordinary dream, but I said that I would be looking out that window at nine o'clock this morning. And so I was. And when I saw you fumble at that first gate and then come through the second, I knew for sure you were the one the Lord was sending to bring us the truth. That's why I opened the door so quickly!"

The woman was so overcome with joy that she burst into tears. When she recovered to some extent, Abe said, "Now I'll tell you my story!"

He told her how the voice had whispered to him to go over the hill and give his message at the house he'd find there. "This book I have contains the truth you've been looking for," Abe continued. "As you read it you may be led into paths you've never dreamed of. For instance, you will learn that the Lord wants you to keep the seventh day holy instead of Sunday."

"He does?" the woman exclaimed. "I've always wondered why people kept Sunday when the Bible says that the seventh day is the Sabbath. Are there any people who keep the seventh day? Do you?"

"Yes," Abe replied, "I was born into a family that keeps the seventh day. As a church we are called Seventh-day Adventists."

"And it tells about it in that book?" she asked. "Then I must have one. I'll pay for it right away, and I want that book just as soon as you can get it here!"

Abe made out the order, and told her he would mail it to the Book and Bible House right away, asking that they send her the book at once. After a wonderful visit and prayer, Abe went on his way.

Throughout the rest of that summer the memory of that incident would cheer him, for sales were few and far between. Finally it was time for him to go back to school. Abe added up his sales, paid his tithe, settled his bills—and had thirty-one dollars left.

There's no use even going to register, he thought. Thirty dollars won't even pay my registration fee. But the voice whispered again in his ear, "Abe, go on and register! The Lord still has thirty days to get the next payment for you."

Abe went to register. At the business office he found that the first payment was thirty dollars. He had that much! He even had one dollar left over. The next payment would not be due for thirty days.

As he stood at the cashier's window, a sudden hearty clap on the shoulder nearly sent him to his knees. A voice boomed out, "Abe, would you like a job?"

Resentful over the force of the blow, Abe answered irritably, without looking around, "Of course I would! I'm always ready for a job!" Then he looked over his shoulder into the face of the president of the school.

"Fine," the man smiled, "Come on into my office and I'll tell you what I have in mind."

When the president and Abe were seated in the office, the man continued, "The Board met last night. They voted to ask you to take charge of the school plant, overseeing all the building. You'd be in charge of the janitorial work and everything. Do you want the job?"

"I certainly do," Abe responded, even as he was wondering if it would pay enough to take care of his tuition.

The President went on, "The board also voted that your wages would be your tuition, your fees, and your food and room as well. How does that sound?"

"It sounds wonderful! It's an answer to prayer," Abe said happily. As he left the office, that one lone dollar in his pocket felt like a million!

Sadly the men watched as their beloved "Portal" burned wildly. They prayed in simple faith that God would not let the boat be destroyed. When they rose from their knees it looked as though a mighty snuffer came down over the boat and put the fire out.

Chapter 21
Kata Rangoso

Kata Rangoso, the first really great man among the native Adventist leaders of the Solomon Islands, was wholly dedicated to God. The Lord used him in a mighty way, and his influence on the native Christians was strong. He inspired strong faith in God and the power of prayer in all those who came in contact with him. The following account about his life is pieced together from a large amount of information gleaned from authentic sources such as historical records in the Heritage Room of the Loma Linda University library, from personal memories of the compiler and some of her friends, and from the stories told by those who worked with him.

Kata Rangoso came to the United States for the General Conference session of Seventh-day Adventists in 1936. He was a striking picture to American eyes. There he was, walking the halls of the convention center in San Francisco with his large, bare, black feet. Those widespread toes were too large to be comfortable in shoes. His feet were built to walk bare on the jungle floor of the Solomon Islands.

A conventional blue serge suit coat with a white shirt and tie worked well for Kata Rangoso. But below that serge suit coat was a plain straight skirt reaching below his knees. No conventional pants could possibly fit his body.

His smiling Christian face and kind eyes, out of which flowed the love of God for everyone, drew the children to him like a magnet. While the grown-up people were talking to him, the children stood in circles around him to gaze up into his kind face with that halo of curly hair on his head.

After the General Conference was over, Kata Rangoso spent some time visiting Pacific Union College, at Angwin, California, where the summer session was in progress. He had a good time with the young people there, for he was mission-educated, and an ordained minister in the Solomon Islands.

Kata Rangoso's father, chief Tatuga of Marovo in the Solomon Islands, was just emerging from heathen darkness in 1902. He was out fishing and decided to defy the spirits by refraining from the use of the usual devil strings. To his delight, he had a full catch of fish. When he arrived home that day, he discovered his new little son had been born in his absence. He called his son Kata Rangoso, which means "No devil strings."

When Kata was twelve years old, pioneer missionary G. E. Jones urged chief Tatuga to let him take Kata and educate him at the mission school at Sasaghana. The lad learned rapidly, and for a time served as a private secretary to the mission director. Then, at age nineteen, he was sent out as a teacher to a village. Later he gained experience serving for many years as assistant to the superintendents.

The work in the Solomon Islands had begun to go well, but not too long after the General Conference session the war broke out, and the Japanese moved rapidly toward the islands to conquer them. When the time came for the foreign missionaries to be evacuated, they all decided that Kata Rangoso was the man to take charge of the mission work in their absence.

As the Japanese approached, the three mission launches, the Portal, the G. P. Jones, and the Dandavata were resting in the quiet Marovo lagoon, waiting for instructions from Kata Rangoso.

The signal came. A canoe pulled in, and a native shouted breathlessly in Pidgin English: *"Jap man e come! Im e come big fellow ship. You go one time quick."*

Immediately the crews in the three mission launches hurried to start their motors and flee with them to Australia, there to remain until after the war. The G. P. Jones and the Dandavata started, but the Portal stalled. A shout went up.

The crew of the Portal knew of a backup plan. Rather than leaving the ship in the Japanese military's hands, they were to destroy it. So they took two drums of gasoline, poured it on the boat, and as they left, they tossed in a match. They hurriedly went to one of the other launches, climbed aboard, and steamed away to safety.

The men on the shore watched sadly as their beloved Portal burned wildly. Kata said to them in their native Marovo language, "The boat belongs to God. Perhaps if we pray, He will not let it burn."

So they all dropped to their knees in the sand and prayed in simple faith for their boat, and if it pleased God, to stop the fire and not let it burn. Then they stood up and watched a wonderful sight. It looked to them as though a mighty snuffer came down over their boat and completely put out the fire. Joyfully they jumped into their canoe and went out to inspect it.

Sure enough, the fire had been put out so quickly that there appeared not to be any permanent damage at all. There was only a lot of soot and a little scorched paint on the outside of the cabin.

They must move quickly now. They knew of a secret inlet hidden by brush at the mouth of a small river that entered the lagoon. They pulled the Portal into that inlet and took it upstream far enough that the jungle growth completely hid it from sight.

No one would be able to discover it unless he knew where to look. Then they returned to the beach and removed all traces of their entrance. Nothing remained but to simply wait for the Japanese navy to come.

When the Japanese ships steamed in and found that the mission launches had escaped, they were angry, but they could do nothing about it. Soon they left.

Once the coast was completely cleared and it was safe to work, Kata gathered his men together and told them: "If they ever do find the Portal we want to be sure that they cannot use it." So they went again to the Portal's hiding place and completely dismantled the engine. Every bolt and screw was laid out. Then Kata said, "We will each take some of the pieces and hide them. Each man will know exactly where his pieces are hidden. When the war is over, we will gather all these parts, put them together, and it will work again."

So each man took charge of some of the pieces and went off to hide them at some secret place in the jungle. Some of them went into holes in trees and other unlikely places. Each man carefully memorized exactly where he had placed his share of the precious boat.

Now came a period of struggle for the people of the Solomon Islands. In the United States we heard stories of air battles over the jungles. Japanese and American fighter planes shot each other down. When the Americans were shot down, they were rescued by what the press called the "Fuzzy Wuzzy Angels." Some of the fighter pilots returned home to tell a strange story.

Kata Rangoso organized his natives into rescue teams. With their incredible eyesight, they could spot falling fliers with their parachutes, and they could tell where they were going to land. The islanders usually reached the stranded pilots long before the enemy could find them.

If the airmen were wounded, Kata's men carried them to their hideout and nursed them back to health, completely hidden from the enemy. If they could walk away, they were led to a safe place where they were fed and taken care of until they could somehow be sent home to America. After the war was over, it was learned that about 200 Allied soldiers had been rescued and cared for by these native people.

In the early days of the Japanese invasion, Kata himself went through a real trial. The chief officer of a detachment of Allied troops became jittery as the battle began to go against them. The officer felt that the indigenous people, including Kata, should do his every command. The natives complied as well as they could.

Then the Sabbath came. The officer ordered Kata to do things his conscience would not allow. He commanded him to work on the Sabbath as on other days. Kata explained politely why he could not do it. The commander became angry and laid him across a barrel, and the order was given to whip him on his bare back. Again he faced the officer who asked him if he would work on that day. When Rangoso politely answered "no", he was knocked to the ground.

When he came to, Rangoso was again ordered to work on the Sabbath. When he again refused, the officer gave an order to a soldier to shoot him. Kata did not flinch. The officer began to shout, "One, two, three, fire!" But the rifle wouldn't fire. Enraged he tried again. "One, two, three, fire!" Again, the weapon wouldn't fire. He tried a third time, "One, two, th...", but the officer stuttered and just couldn't get out the word "three."

Rangoso was not shot, but together with another pastor named Lundi, was taken to a prison compound and left there. The Christian nationals were worried, and a council of church leaders was held. They decided that on a certain night, as the moon came over the mountains, they would gather wherever they were and pray for Kata Rangoso and his companion.

The message was sent out by jungle drum. On the designated night, a tall man with a big bunch of keys came to the gate of the prison compound, took hold of the lock, turned the key and opened the gate, calling out, "Rangoso!"

"Yes, sir."

Then the tall man shouted, "Lundi!"

"Yes, sir."

"Come here."

The two prisoners rose from the ground, where they had been trying to sleep, and went to the gate. The tall man took them by the arm, let them quietly through the gate, locked it, then led them down the path that went toward the beach. When they were in sight of the water, the tall man paused and said, "Go down to the beach. There you will find a canoe. Go home."

The two surprised men walked forward a few steps, and there, in plain sight, was a canoe with paddles gleaming in the moonlight. They turned to thank the one who had released them, but the path was empty.

No one ever found the tall man or the keys that were used to unlock the prison gate that night. The guard said that the keys to the jail were never off the peg in the guardhouse that night. But the faithful believers of the South Seas know that God answered prayer as He did for His people of old.

When the war was over and the missionaries returned, they went first to Marovo Lagoon. There the native Christians received them joyfully and said, "Come, we will show you the Portal."

The missionaries had gotten word from the British that the Portal had been destroyed. The natives only smiled and said, "Come and see."

So they followed them up the little inlet to the hidden Portal. The missionaries looked at it in amazement. "But there is no engine!"

Kata, smiling mysteriously, and with a twinkle in his eyes, quietly spoke a command to his men, "Go bring all the engine parts."

They scattered into the jungle, and in a short while returned with all the parts of the engine, down to the last nut, bolt, and screw. Then began the tedious job of putting the engine back together again. The missionaries were amazed that not a single piece was missing!

At last it was time for the big test. Would it run?

They tried to start the engine. Off it went with a big flourish, just as if it had never been taken apart. The Portal went on with its work serving the mission, just as it had before the war.

As for Kata Rangoso, he still had years to serve as a leader in the Solomon Islands. From 1953 to 1957 he was president of the Western Solomon Island Mission. During that time he came again as a delegate to the 1954 General Conference session in San Francisco.

In addition to being a big help in the work of translating the entire Bible into the Marovo language, Kata toured the Australasian Division. He lectured in conferences, missions and churches. He was loved wherever he went.

In a message to his people shortly before his death in 1964 Kata Rangoso wrote: "I have tried to help finish the Master's work. That has been my one desire. To the national workers I would say, 'do not let down the work God has given into your hands, but uphold the torch of truth.'"

Chapter 22

Answer at 3:25

Elder A.F. Tarr grew up in South Africa. From there he went as a missionary to India. He and his wife had been on furlough, and at the time of this story they were returning to India. After visiting old friends, they were ready to take the ship and finish their journey. Suddenly it looked impossible to go on, but prayer solved the problem. The following account by Mary Ogle appeared in *Guide*, February 15, 1967.

The time was exactly twenty-five minutes after three o'clock in the afternoon. The day was Thursday, May 19. The year was 1949. The place was the city of Durban in South America.

Elder A.F. Tarr remembers the time, because he looked at his watch as he and his wife rose from their knees in their hotel room. They had just prayed that God would solve the mystery. They prayed that He would find the thief and that He would bring back the valuable briefcase and handbag containing all his money and their Bibles.

Most important of all, they prayed for the return of their passport with the very important paper marked "Prohibited Immigrant, Permission to enter India." Without that statement, signed by the Indian government, the Tarrs could not return to their home in India, where Elder Tarr was secretary-treasurer of the Southern Asia Division of Seventh-day Adventists, with headquarters in the city of Poona.

Elder and Mrs. Tarr had arrived in Durban only a short while before that memorable hour of 3:25. They were on their way to India after a trip to America, and had come by way of Africa to visit their old home. In their European car they had toured sections of the country, visiting family and friends. Now the time was drawing near when they must take ship again. They were booked to sail from Durban for Bombay the coming Sunday afternoon.

Before going to their hotel, they had decided to stop for lunch at an attractive little restaurant. Parking their car across the street from the restaurant, Elder Tarr placed his briefcase and Mrs. Tarr's handbag in the center of the car, surrounding them with what he hoped would look like uninteresting packages. After carefully locking the door, they crossed the street to the restaurant and enjoyed a delicious lunch. They returned to the car only to find that someone had skillfully opened the car door, stolen the briefcase and the handbag, and escaped.

They called the police. Soon two policemen came roaring up on their motorcycles. They looked the car over, saw the tiny hole in the glass on the front door, shook their heads and said, "Sorry we can't hold out much hope for catching this kind of thief, Mr. Tarr. But bring the car down to the police station for fingerprints, and we'll see what we can do."

After the visit to the police station, the Tarrs went to their hotel, and there they knelt down and told their troubles to the only One who could help them. "You called us to do a work in India. You know we can't go back into that country without our passport and the special permit, so please help us to find the things we have lost."

As they rose from their knees, Elder Tarr looked at his watch. It was 3:25.

At ten o'clock that night the telephone rang in their room. "This is the police station calling. We think we have found your belongings. Will you come down the first thing in the morning and identify them?" Again Elder Tarr and Mrs. Tarr knelt. This time they said, "Thank you, Lord."

Like a couple of excited children, they walked into the police station the next morning. Sure enough, there were all their belongings. Some of them were considerably mussed up, but there were all the important papers, the money, the handbag, the Bibles, the passport, *and* the re-entry permit!

Elder Tarr thought he could just pick up his things and be on his way. "Oh no," said the chief of police. "You cannot touch these things. They must be held as evidence in the magistrate's court." He put everything back into the briefcase and stamped it with the government stamp seal.

"When is the next session of court?" asked Elder Tarr.

"Monday morning."

"Monday! But I must sail on Sunday."

"Sorry, but it is not possible to hold a session of court before Monday. It is already Friday, and there is no court on Saturday or Sunday." That closed the matter as far as the chief of police was concerned.

"Let's go to the steamship company," suggested Mrs. Tarr. "Maybe they will have a ship going a little later."

As they walked into the office of the steamship company, the manager greeted them. "Oh, Mr. Tarr, I've been trying to get in touch with you. We have received word that your ship will not sail until Monday afternoon at 2:30."

"Thank you, Lord," breathed Elder Tarr again.

The court was crowded on Monday morning. Elder Tarr was ushered to the front of the room and seated alongside three sullen-looking young men. The first witness called to testify was a young woman nineteen years of age. This is the story she told the court:

"On Thursday afternoon I was sewing by the window in our third-floor apartment. At about 3:25 I looked out the window and saw three men, carrying a brief case and other parcels, enter our apartment building. I immediately felt impressed that they were carrying stolen goods. I went across the street to my father's garage and called the police. I told them I thought they would find stolen goods in our apartment building."

"Do you think you could identify those three men?" the judge asked.

"Yes, sir," she answered. "There they are," and she pointed her finger at the three young men sitting beside Elder Tarr, which caused him to turn and take a second look at his seatmates.

Then the police officer testified that, in response to this telephone call, he and another officer had gone to the apartment house. They found the three young men in a room with a fire going and with the papers and other stolen goods scattered on a table. They were preparing to burn what they did not want.

Court was dismissed at one o'clock, and Elder Tarr was given back his personal belongings. A friend hurried him and Mrs. Tarr through the traffic. They reached the dock and boarded the ship with a little time to spare before it pulled away from Durban's wharf bound for Bombay.

Elder Tarr never learned why the ship's sailing was delayed for twenty-four hours, but it was most unusual for a mail steamer to be delayed. He thinks he knows who gave the sailing orders. It must have been the "Master of earth and sea and sky."

That briefcase has accompanied Elder Tarr to many countries of the world in the years since then. It still shows the scar where the seal was attached. Among his souvenirs, Elder Tarr carries the passport and the paper declaring that he was at one time a "Prohibited Immigrant" with special permission to re-enter India. He carries these as reminders that "Heaven is only a prayer away," and that God fulfilled His promise to him on Thursday, May 19, 1949, at 3:25 in the afternoon.

Chapter 23
The Prayer and Faith of Inani

This story is based on a report given by Bill Liversidge at a camp meeting in the United States. Bill Liversidge, who was a missionary from Australia to New Guinea for many years, had a good friend by the name of Inani. Inani was the captain of the mission boat that traveled up and down the coast of Papua New Guinea, serving the various mission stations. At the time, Bill was the pastor of a church in Port Moresby. Inani really walked with the Lord Jesus day by day, and his faith was an inspiration to all he met.

As Inani piloted the mission boat along that coast of New Guinea, he loved to watch the coral reef and the colorful fish swimming in the tropical waters. And, like all of his friends, Inani loved to go spear fishing. He had fashioned his own spear gun, which he used whenever he had a chance. It was rusty, of course, from the salt water. It had a barbed point and was quite long. His gun was triggered without a guard so he could handle it quickly.

One afternoon when the mission boat was ahead of schedule, Inani decided to go spear fishing for an hour or two. He saw a very fine fish, and got it with his spear gun. When he was pulling it in, it slipped off the spear, and he saw his prize escaping, even though it was wounded.

Quickly Inani reset his gun and let it float in the water as usual. He dived in after the fish, and he got it. But as he returned to the surface, his spear gun sank to an out-cropping piece of coral, and hit the trigger. The gun shot off with its usual velocity, and caught Inani right under the jaw bone. The spear entered his head, passed through between the eyes, and came out the frontal lobe at the top of his head. It protruded about three inches.

Imagine the consternation of the crew when they saw their captain emerging from the water with that spear through his head! They helped Inani clamber aboard, then quickly turned their boat and went to the nearest mission station, which was two hours away.

While they called for the plane to come from Port Moresby, the missionary sawed off the long protruding bottom of the spear with a common hacksaw. By the time the plane got there and took Inani to Port Moresby, it had been six hours since the accident. Inani was conscious through the whole ordeal, but he had lost a lot of blood and was getting weaker.

When Pastor Liversidge picked him up at the airport and took a look at him, he thought, "There isn't much of a chance for this man!" When they got to the hospital, he took Inani's hand and said, "Inani, I will pray for you, for it is plain that there isn't much help for you unless the Lord works for you."

Inani spoke: "Pastor, I have already talked it over with Jesus, and he told me I would be all right."

Pastor Liversidge said, "Well, if you have already talked to the Lord and He told you that, there isn't more I can do, but we will pray anyway." So there in the hospital they had prayer together.

Soon they came to get Inani to take him to have the spear removed from his head. Before they could start the surgery, they had to push the spear the rest of the way through his head because of the barbs. While they worked to get the spear out, the doctor said to Pastor Liversidge, "I don't believe there is any possible chance that this man will survive the surgery, and if he does, he will be nothing but a cabbage."

The pastor answered, "Well, I will pray anyway and we will see what tomorrow brings." Then the pastor left and went home, leaving the doctor in charge.

Early the next morning, Pastor Liversidge returned to the hospital and said to a nurse, "Could I go in and see Inani?"

"Sure," the nurse answered.

When Pastor Liversidge entered Inani's room, he was surprised to see him sitting up in bed. "Inani, you should be lying down," he said.

"No, I'm feeling fine."

"But Inani, you've just had major surgery, and I'd prefer if you would lie down." After talking with Inani for awhile, Pastor Liversidge walked out of the room and down the hall in search of the doctor.

"Doctor, that man does not look very sick to me," he said.

"What did you pray last night?" asked the doctor.

Pastor Liversidge said, "It isn't what I prayed, Doctor. Inani told me last night before I prayed that he had talked it over with Jesus and He had told him, he would be all right."

Inani was out of the hospital in four days, and back to work on the mission boat seven days after the accident. The Pastor told us that all Inani has today is the scars below his jaw and on the top of his head where the spear came out. He has absolutely no damage of any kind to his body or his mind. The doctor gave the Inani X-rays to the pastor, for he said no one would believe his story unless they saw the X-rays.

God is worthy of praise for honoring pure and simple faith as exercised by men such as Inani.

Chapter 24
Manna Fell in Africa in 1939

In 1939 an isolated mission station in Africa was supplied with food in answer to prayer. All food reserves were gone, and the food that God supplied was thought to be manna. The story did not become generally known in America until 1946 when Pastor E. L. Cardy came home on furlough, bringing with him a sample of manna to Washington, D.C. While he was there, he spoke in the Sligo Church and had a box of the manna so those who wished could take a look.

Lora Clement, who was at that time editor of *The Youth's Instructor*, wrote the story as she had heard it in church, and published it on the editorial page of the December 10, 1946, *The Youth's Instructor*. Later E. C. Cardy wrote the story for *Signs of the Times*. Then it was reprinted by the *Voice of Prophecy News* in January 1948. From the facts given in these sources the story is retold here.

In 1924 Pastor and Mrs. W. H. Anderson, pioneer missionaries to Africa, pushed up into interior Angola, enduring many hardships of travel. They came to an area where no missionaries had ever been. The villages were ruled by superstition and witchcraft. The couple established their mission station and began to give the everlasting gospel to the heathen near them, then planted their own gardens to eat as the natives did.

Gradually many were won to Christ, and many came to the mission school. Christian families moved there and became part of the evangelistic work. The work grew so large and the native help was so efficient that the white missionaries left it completely in the hands of the native workers. By 1939 there were about 400 people in the Central Angola mission, which included many outstations and schools.

Because the rains failed to come on time, the crops failed, and the food was all gone. The director's wife called the people together to pray. She told them, "We have run out of food. We will ask the Lord for our daily bread."

She read the promises of God and spoke to the people of the manna He had sent the children of Israel who were traveling in the desert. She said, "If necessary, God can even send us manna as He did them." Then all the people knelt in simple faith asking the Lord to send them food.

When they arose from their knees, the director's little girl, about five years old, wandered outside. She soon came back in with her hands full of some white stuff, which she was eating. When they asked what she was eating she said, "It is manna." Then she told this story.

When she went out, several Europeans were standing there. They said to her, "Little girl, your prayers have been heard and God has sent you manna. See it is all over the ground. Pick up some. It is good." So the child picked it up and went back into the house eating it.

Hearing this, the people all rushed out. The manna, which looked like the Bible described it, was all over the ground. On eating it, it tasted just like the Bible said it did. It was filling and satisfying to eat and apparently a balanced food. The European men were gone. No one but the little child ever saw them.

The director's wife suggested that the people get vessels from their homes and gather the manna up. This they did and found it on all the forty acres of the cleared mission property but nowhere else.

The director, Carlos Sequeseque was away visiting some distant mission schools and had been gone for several weeks at the time of the manna incident. Mrs. Sequeseque immediately sent word to her husband, bidding him, "Hurry home. A miracle has happened." So he came home and saw it.

The food fell for three days. No one ever saw it fall but when the morning sun dried the dew, there it was. It did not spoil, as the manna of the wilderness in Bible times did. This manna kept, just as the pot of manna did that was kept in the ark of the covenant. The manna that Pastor Cardy brought to America had been kept in Capetown for seven years and it was still as fresh as ever.

The manna that the natives gathered during those three days was enough to last them until the rains came again and a new crop of maize was harvested.

When Carlos Sequeseque sent in his report to the mission headquarters, he included a box of manna with his letter, telling them it first fell on April 19, 1939. The mission officers tasted it and became convinced it answered the description given in the Bible.

In 1952 I was teaching the first grade class in the eight grade church school in Lodi, California. One Sabbath I walked down to visit the Primary division. The leader asked me to tell a story, and I decided to tell the story of the manna that fell in Africa in 1939, and of the sample coming to America in 1946. The story being finished, I went up to attend my class in the Senior Sabbath School upstairs.

After church I was walking the few blocks to my home. I soon became aware of hurrying feet behind me. It was the long stride of a man and the running steps of a child. I turned to see one of my first grade girls, Caroline, and her tall father trying to catch up with me. The father said, "Mrs. Tupper, Caroline has something she wants to tell you."

Caroline told me that her grandmother, who lives in Washington, D.C. and attends the Sligo Church, was there when Pastor Cardy told the story, and she was one who walked up to see the real manna. The grandmother wrote and told Caroline and her parents, and when she visits, she tells them the story again and again.

An urgent voice commanded Elder Williams to go to New York City that night. The next morning, he heard the raucous voice of the newsboy: "Extra! Extra! Banks closed! Extra! Banks closed nationwide!" Tears came to his eyes as he realized what God had done for the church.

Chapter 25

God Was Ready the Day the Banks Closed

Franklin D. Roosevelt was elected president of the United States of America in the fall of 1932. Between that time and his March 4, 1933, inauguration, banks were closing all over our country. Many people lost their life's savings and their homes. Many were out of work. Those who lived where they could raise some food were the most secure.

At the time of that crisis, the Adventist world headquarters was in Washington, D.C. The economic and financial difficulties of the country affected the church's work, too, but God knew what was coming. He had a dedicated man in charge at this time whom He used to save the Lord's money and keep the work going in all the world field.

The following story by Emma Howell Cooper tells the details just as they occurred. As a secretary of the Adventist Youth Department, she worked in the same building in which W. H. Williams worked. This complete account was published in the September 13, 1979, *The Review and Herald*.

A thousand dollars is a lot of money to keep in a small safe. (According to the CPI inflation calculator, a thousand dollars in 1933 had the same buying power as $17,887 in 2013.) Yet, W. H. Williams, undertreasurer of the General Conference, asked his secretary to place ten $100 bills in an envelope, date it, mark the amount, and put the envelope into the office safe. In subsequent weeks the secretary stuffed, dated, and marked other envelopes, also storing them in the safe.

Being a keen financier, Elder Williams understood the currencies of many lands. The Lord needed just such a man in 1933. That was a time of the Great Depression. Funds were scarce, and many people were going hungry. The world budget of the church had been cut at the annual meeting, and a general feeling of concern prevailed.

Elder Williams had charge of the flow of denominational funds in and out of the General Conference with respect to both the world field and the North American

Division. Because of this, he did his banking not only in Takoma Park and downtown Washington, D.C., but in New York City, as well.

The $1,000 amounts Elder Williams directed his secretary, Chester Rogers, to put into the office safe were funds he had withdrawn periodically from the General Conference account at the Takoma Park Bank. His secretary wondered why he made these withdrawals.

The drawing of cash from the bank and then storing it in the office safe was not the only strange thing that the secretary had noticed Elder Williams doing lately. He had recently written letters to the overseas divisions urging them to send in their budget requests for the next Annual Council. This was far in advance of the usual schedule. Why all the rush?

Elder Williams then further complicated the situation by asking Mr. Rogers to drive him to Union Station in downtown Washington so he could take the midnight train for an unscheduled trip to New York City. Of course, Elder Williams frequently went to New York City to arrange to send mission funds by cable to the various division offices, but this time it was fully ten days before the date such a trip normally would have been scheduled. Why did he need to go to New York City that night? Mr. Rogers wondered, but asked no questions.

A few days later, in a regular morning chapel service at the General Conference office, Elder Williams told the office a story that made a lasting impression on everyone present. Here it is as told in his own words:

It was closing time on March 2. People were rushing home from work while I sat alone in my office enjoying the quiet hush after a busy day. Because my wife was not at home, there was no need for me to hurry to an empty house. "I will go home and go to bed early," I mused to myself.

Just then, there was a pressure on my shoulder, and a clear voice commanded: "Go to New York City tonight."

I sat up and braced myself in my chair. Then I bowed my head and prayed, "Lord, I have no authority to transact business in New York City at this time. What am I to do when I get there?"

The pressure continued: "Go!"

I was tired. I dreaded a late-night trip to Union Station by streetcar. Had Chester Rogers gone yet? Stepping outside my office, I met my faithful secretary. "Chester, will you take me to the train tonight?" I asked. To this he agreed without question.

Early the next morning I arrived in New York City. I prayed that the Lord would keep me from any improper transactions that day. Why was I there, anyway? As the morning advanced, the answer came clearly: "Go to the two banks and send the mission money to each division."

But this was too early in the month, I reasoned with the Lord. However, there seemed to be no alternative.

When the banks opened that Friday morning, I found myself at the first bank, facing the teller who normally handled our mission transactions. He knew our schedule. I wondered if he would straighten me out. But the teller did not raise so much as an eyebrow at seeing me that day, and at such an early hour. When I told him that I wished to send the mission funds to the usual places, he replied, "Yes, Mr. Williams, I'll be happy to care of that."

After checking to be sure he had the correct addresses, I gave him a list of the various amounts to send to each division. As I did so I found myself saying, "In fact, I'd like to send three times our regular amount in each case, please."

With a telescopic view my mind's eye could see the figures of our accounts. Yes, we had enough in the bank to cover three months' appropriations for each place, but it certainly would leave little in reserve!

The teller indicated that he would carry out my wishes. After turning away from the window, I stepped back again. "You'll be sure to attend to this at once, please?" I urged.

"Yes, of course, Mr. Williams, it will be the next thing I do," replied the teller.

When I arrived at the bank that morning I was trembling so much that I could scarcely walk. But inside the bank all my quaking and fears vanished. Out on the street the shaking returned. How could I ever explain to the General Conference officers what I had just done without their authorization?

Again I felt the pressure on my shoulder, and more words: "Go to the other bank and send those funds now." The voice sounded as though there was no time to lose!

Again I followed the instruction. At the second bank I again met a cordial reception and I transferred the mission funds in exactly the same manner I had at the first bank, not forgetting to caution the teller that the money should be cabled at once, and receiving the same assurance as at the first bank.

Then the next step became clear to me: I must cable the divisions and say, "Conserve funds. Letter follows." Having attended to this, I suddenly realized that I was completely exhausted.

It was a relief to think that now I could take the train back to Washington and the streetcar to Takoma Park. I would arrive in midafternoon, and the General Conference offices would be closed. However, there would be many Seventh-day Adventists scurrying here and there on the streets, preparing for the Sabbath. I preferred not to meet anyone.

Since the streetcar line ends in front of a shopping area, I wondered if anyone would tell me that he had needed me in the office that morning. In weariness and apprehension I prayed: "Lord, let me get home alone. Don't let me be obliged to talk with anyone when I get back. Please help me!"

I must have dozed a bit. All at once I realized that we were being switched onto a siding. Soon the conductor explained that there had been a wreck ahead, and it would be some time before the track was cleared. When finally I arrived at Union Station in downtown Washington and then made my way to Takoma Park by streetcar, it was already dark.

The streets were deserted. I walked the few blocks to my home on Carroll Avenue without meeting a person I knew. Soon I was in bed, after praying that the Lord would grant me a good night's rest and would prevent my awakening on the Sabbath with my mind in a turmoil over the past day's activities.

The Lord granted my request, for I slept soundly. In fact, Sabbath was well along before I awakened to find the sun shining across my bed. It was March 4, 1933, and it was the day Franklin D. Roosevelt was to be inaugurated as United States President. For a moment I lay there. How good it was to relax!

Then, through my open window came the raucous voice of a newsboy: "EXTRA! EXTRA! Banks closed! Extra! Banks closed nationwide! "

I sprang from my bed. In my pajamas I rushed to the door for a newspaper. I had to know what had happened! And there it was; a two-inch-high black headline proclaiming: "Banks Closed Nationwide!" As I began to realize what this meant, tears came to my eyes, making it difficult for me to read.

I was deeply humbled to realize that the Lord had used me to save most of our mission funds. I spent the rest of the Sabbath alone with God, praising the Lord. I prayed that He would always keep me humble in His service.

Immediately after sundown my telephone rang sharply. It was Elder J. L. Shaw, our General Conference treasurer. He was calling a meeting of the Treasury personnel immediately in his office. "You have heard the news," he said. "What will we do to support our missionaries?" Then he hung up before I could answer.

I noticed that as the treasurers entered Elder Shaw's office, everyone was tense, and all were talking in subdued tones. All were especially concerned for our overseas workers. "With the banks closed there will be no funds to support the missionaries in the field, neither will there be money with which to bring them home," Elder Shaw explained to us.

At that point I requested permission to speak. I quietly related to them my story.

We had a prayer season that evening instead of a business meeting. Instead of agonized prayers for help, there were prayers of praise and gratitude for God's wonderful guidance. Nor did we forget to beseech Him to keep us humble in the future. Oh, that He might always lead us as He had in this instance, we prayed.

As we rose from our knees, someone remarked that we had been so concerned for our overseas missionaries that we had given no thought to the needs of our workers at headquarters. How would we provide for them? How long would the banks be closed?

Then I remembered the $1,000 items in the little safe in my office. Quickly we counted the envelopes. With care there would be enough cash with which to meet our payroll for the next three months—the same length of time for which we had sent funds the day before to the overseas divisions.

When Elder Williams sat down that morning it was evident that the congregation had been greatly moved. Thousands of small banks went permanently out of business on March 4, 1933. Many large banks and some small, stronger banks did not open again until after a panic-filled period had passed—a period of three months. During that time it was not possible to send funds out of the United States.

During this time, the Seventh-day Adventist Mission Board did not recall one missionary. Neither did the General Conference find it necessary to borrow funds in order to carry on its work. The payroll for the General Conference was on schedule during the time the banks were closed, paid from the dated and marked envelopes in the little safe in Elder Williams' office.

Chapter 26
Remarkable Answer to Prayer

A pressing bill had to be paid, and no money was available. But the required amount arrived in the mail just in time to meet the need. The Lord answered prayer. The story, written by Helen F. Smith, was published in *The Review and Herald*, on August 17, 1961.

Not long ago in New York City, a prayer for help received a remarkable answer by the same gracious God who heard the cry of the widow in Elisha's day and enabled her to meet the insistent demands of her creditors.

Austin E. Butler, business manager of the New York Center, has struggled against seemingly overwhelming financial problems as did his predecessors since the institution opened. He often has had the unhappy task of appeasing creditors.

Among the unpaid bills on a recent Thursday was one for $1,140, which Elder Butler was urgently requested to pay by the first of the following week. He promised to do his best. Then, knowing no place to turn for the money, he left his office and drove to Long Island. As he drove, Elder Butler asked the Lord for help. At last, feeling reassured, though he had no tangible answer, he turned back to the City.

The next morning, as he opened his mail, Elder Butler slit open one of the center's printed return envelopes provided for gifts. Out fell a fifty dollar bill. The envelope bore only a Bronx postmark. A second identical envelope contained two fifty dollar bills, and a third held five one hundred dollar bills. He now had $650 with no clue as to the identity of the sender.

The following Monday the morning mail brought another envelope with five one hundred dollar bills. Elder Butler now had a total of $1,150 in fifty and one hundred dollar bills, in identical envelopes, without any identification.

Like the girl who prayed for Peter's release from prison, and then found it hard to believe that he was at the door, Elder Butler's first reaction was to wonder whether someone had made a mistake. He took the money to the bank to be sure it was not counterfeit. When deposited at last to the center's account, the anonymous gifts covered the bill that had caused such concern.

For the center's staff; this token of God's willingness to answer prayer has been a sobering challenge to a deeper love for, and dependence upon their heavenly Father in meeting the overwhelming problems of evangelizing New York City.

Chapter 27
From the Heart

Up in Iceland, the Lord provided the exact amount of money self-supporting missionaries needed to pay for the rent of a Bible school building and for an accordion that was to be used in the school's programs. This story, written by Lois May Cuhel, appeared in *Guide* on September 10, 1976.

Father shook his head slowly, "I'd certainly like to buy you an accordion, Gary," he said. "But $239 is a lot more money than we have."

Gary Magneson understood. He lived in Iceland, where his parents were self-supporting missionaries. The Lord always met every need for the family, but at times, when you are a thirteen-year-old boy, you can't help wishing and hoping for a certain specific thing now and then, just like other boys your age do.

There were some special needs in this Icelandic community. Gary's parents needed money for a Bible school for children. Mother and Father knew that making it possible for young children and teenagers to hear the Gospel was more important than an accordion. Gary knew it too.

But he peeked just once more at the picture of the accordion in the catalog. What a wonderful little instrument! It was just the right size and color—a beautiful green. He could help father and mother in the Bible school by playing for the singing, if only it were his.

Finally Gary put the catalog aside, and his thoughts of the green accordion faded a little. But one day in a downtown store window he saw it again. The just-right green accordion. It was exactly like the one in the catalog.

Gary hurried home. "Father!" he called, "Know what I saw in a store window? An accordion just like the one in the catalog. And it's on sale! It's not $239, it's only $189."

Father smiled, but again he shook his head, "You know how much we would like to get that accordion for you. And we certainly would like to have you play for Bible classes. But I'm afraid that $189 is still more than we can afford. In fact: We don't have even $50 to pay for our Bible study building."

Gary understood, and he might have forgotten all about the accordion if a certain letter hadn't come just two days later. It had a foreign stamp on it, and it had come from Hong Kong, halfway around the world. Miss May Clyde, a friend of Mother's and Father's, sent the letter. She was a missionary and had been in Hong Kong, China, for more than forty years. Amazingly, the Lord put it into her heart to write this letter and enclose something wonderful.

Miss Clyde wrote, "The Lord impressed me to send this money for you," she wrote, "You must have some special need at this time, a need He knows about, although I do not."

Gary looked at the check she had enclosed. It was made out for $100. "The accordion!" he cried. Father smiled, "Do you suppose the Lord spoke to someone halfway around the world in order to give you that accordion?"

"Do you think the one in the store is still on sale?" Gary asked. But then disappointment clouded his face. "But that was $189, even on sale," he remembered. "The check is for only $100."

"Well, we will go down to the store and have a look at it anyway," Father said. "If the Lord really wants you to have it, I am sure He will supply the $89 we still lack."

So downtown they went, Father and Mother, and Gary—to look at the accordion. And what they saw when they came to the store was so wonderful they could scarcely believe their eyes. The manager of the store was putting a sign on the window that very minute, right beside the green accordion. The sign read, "Special sale price, $50."

"Fifty dollars!" Gary exclaimed.

"Fifty dollars!" his father repeated thoughtfully, "And that is the very accordion that was in the catalog for nearly five times as much!"

"The Lord has done it again," Mother smiled, "Here we thought the check was $89 less than we needed for the accordion, yet God has amazingly worked it out so that it is $50 more than enough. And the extra money is just what we need to pay the extra rent for the Bible school. It's just on time, too!"

So that is how God timed matters perfectly. He not only supplied the building where His Word was to be taught, but he helped provide the music as well.

Above Gary's bed is tacked a snapshot of the very special missionary, Miss May Clyde. Though half a world away, and knowing nothing of either the Bible school's need nor Gary's, she became part of a miracle because she loved and obeyed God's whisper in her heart.

Chapter 28
A Miraculous Healing in Malaysia

W. W. R. Lake tells here his own experience of instant healing. His account was published in the September 1, 1955, issue of *These Times*. He had been a missionary in the Far Eastern Division for many years, and had recently moved to Singapore where he was just beginning his work.

The roar of an ancient motorcycle, with accompanying sidecar, pierced the early morning Malayan air. A fellow missionary had started the engine that was to take us on a business trip from Singapore to Kuala Lumpur, 250 miles to the north. Although I had never driven a motorcycle, there was an unspoken understanding between us that he would drive to Kuala Lumpur, and I would drive back.

As our machine chugged its bumpy way northward, I thought of my work in Singapore. I had recently been called as pastor of the Singapore Seventh-day Adventist Church. Unfortunately, because of a lack of funds, the members had been without adequate pastoral attention, and many of them had become discouraged. To stimulate and encourage them, and to bring in new converts, I had begun a series of evangelistic meetings.

My traveling companion guided the cycle unerringly down the unmarked roads, little realizing that his machine would soon figure prominently in a miraculous healing and a heart-warming spiritual recovery.

We arrived at our destination safely, and immediately started to work. Our mission was completed in three days, and we planned to leave early the next morning. Since it was my turn to drive, I thought I had better get a lesson first. The evening before our departure, my friend carefully explained the operating procedure, then blithely told me to go ahead. You could have stirred my knees with a spoon. Summoning up my courage, I climbed aboard and started off.

The machine soon went out of control, and before I realized it, I had careened crazily across the highway and smashed into a huge rock. I was yanked completely out of the saddle and thrown into the air, coming down on the rock's jagged edge. My left hip caught the full impact.

The accident happened around five in the evening. That is the time when doctors and nurses return to their homes from the hospitals. Within a matter of a few minutes, three doctors and two nurses came by and attended to me. An ambulance soon arrived, and I was picked up and taken to the European hospital.

In the meantime, the police asked my companion not to leave Kuala Lumpur. Since my life was hanging in the balance, they thought that if anything should happen to me, as owner of the cycle, he would have to answer.

The reports from the hospital stated that I was not expected to live. X-rays revealed that the left hip and the pelvic bone were completely shattered. Within twenty-four hours complications set in. The first of these was peritonitis. Later I developed a high fever.

Someone told my wife, Clara, what had happened to me. She arrived the next morning, but was not allowed to see me. She soon met the attending surgeon, Dr. Danette, who told her that he held no hope for me. Dr. Danette was an exceedingly good surgeon, but very austere and dogmatic. He was the head of the hospital, and all the other surgeons and physicians gave him a wide berth. His temper was unpredictable.

For the first four or five days I was semiconscious. Drugs and sedatives did not relieve one iota of the pain. It was terrible.

Unknown to me at the time, my missionary friend asked permission of the police department to return to Singapore to get his mission books. He wanted to bring them to Kuala Lumpur and do his work from the station. I believe it was the fifth day that he traveled. The sixth evening there was a prayer meeting in the church in Singapore, beginning at seven thirty.

My companion took charge of the meeting, and explained about the accident. He said there was really no hope, humanly speaking, and called upon the church members to pray. He reviewed Psalm 78 that night, and as a result there was a deep heart-searching among the church members. Sins were put away. The grace of God came very softly and tenderly upon them. Ordinary, simple men and women went down on their knees and prayed that God would not only forgive them, but also make their lives a channel through which His great power, His grace, and His mercy might flow to others, especially to me.

About eight o'clock that night, while these people were praying in Singapore, two nurses in the hospital were tending to me. They rubbed my back with alcohol. They turned me first on one side and then on the other, an operation that took between ten and twelve minutes. Every time a movement was made, I experienced stabbing pain. I was lying now on a waterbed. Sandbags weighing between fifteen and twenty pounds apiece were wedged on either side of me to keep me from moving.

When the nurses again came to turn me over to the left side, my broken side, there came into my whole physical structure a change. My mind became alert. The fogginess of all those drugs, which had rendered my thinking nebulous, vanished away. I was electrified. My brain was clear. My mind was lucid. I wondered what had caused this change. At the same time, while they were turning me over, there was no pain.

When I was turned on my back, the nurses readjusted the pillows and smoothed out the covers. Then they said to me, "You were good this time. What's happened?" I didn't say a word. They said, "Good night."

At nine o'clock the lights were turned out. I lifted the sandbag on my left side and threw it over the bed. It went down with a thud, but apparently nobody heard it. I then turned on my broken side and went to sleep.

I must have slept from nine o'clock that night to six the next morning without a stir. I had not slept for five or six nights because of the pain and inconvenience.

The night nurse on duty, before she left at seven, peered into my face. At the same time I opened my eyes. She said, "You have been sleeping on your broken side all night. You are being reported to Dr. Danette."

That remark made to any patient, or to any member of the staff, meant trouble! But I felt that I could meet the world. I felt that God had heard someone's prayer and had healed me! At the time, of course, I was unaware of the prayer meeting in Singapore.

My temperature was taken, and it was normal. The tenseness and the soreness of my abdomen was gone. I rubbed my side, my fractured hip, and found no pain. I thanked God for what He had done.

Dr. Danette arrived at five minutes to eight. The nurse met him at his car. It was the first time I saw him walk so briskly, so quickly, into my room. When he came in, I said, "Good morning."

He growled, "Morning. The nurse reports to me that you have been sleeping on your fractured hip." I didn't answer. He drew the sheet down and got hold of the hip, at first very gently. He asked, "Is there any pain?"

I said, "No."

Then he applied pressure to the pelvis. He looked at me strangely. "Is there any pain?"

"No."

Then he punched my abdomen where a few hours before I could not stand even the touch of the sheet over me, it was so tender.

"Any pain?" the doctor demanded.
"No pain," I replied.
"When did this happen?"
"When did what happen?"
"When did all this pain cease?"
"Between eight and eight thirty last night."
"How do you account for it?"
"I don't know."
"Who are you?"
"I'm a missionary."
"What church do you belong to?"
"The Seventh-day Adventist Church."

This time the only answer was a grunt. He was puzzled, He went to see some of the other patients. Word got around the hospital that the dying man was alive, free from all pain. There were other physicians and surgeons in the hospital who were acquainted with my case. They came in while Dr. Danette was out to find out how I was getting on. They asked what had happened. I told them. At the end of half an hour, Dr. Danette came back again and examined me in the same way as before. He looked at me a long time.

"When did this happen?" he asked again.
"Between eight and eight thirty last night."
"How did it happen?"
"Well," I said, "after the alcohol rub I felt that I wanted to sleep, and I also felt that there was no pain. I turned on my fractured side because I couldn't sleep on my back. I had a wonderful night, and I feel refreshed."
"Who are you?" he repeated.
"I'm a Seventh-day Adventist missionary."

Dr. Danette walked away. His mind was disturbed. He went around the hospital looking at patients. He was scheduled for an operation about ten, but he came to me again first. He repeated the same questions, looked more puzzled than ever, gave me the same grunt, and went to his surgery.

After the operation, Dr. Danette came in again. It was about ten minutes to twelve when he again examined me, going over the same parts and asking me the same questions. He was more than puzzled as to my religious persuasion, and he always left me with the same grunt. Then he left for lunch.

That afternoon at four he returned, making a beeline to my bed. He again put me through the process of examination, with questions and queries.

"Who are you?"

I said, "I believe I've told you before, but I am a Seventh-day Adventist missionary."

He grunted again and said, "Have you any pain at all?"

"None. You know, doctor, I'm able to wiggle my feet and flex my toes. I can flex my knees."

He said, "You can? Let me see it."

I showed him that movement caused me no distress. He threw the sheet over me and walked away.

Returning from the club that night at ten, Dr. Danette stopped by on his way home. The examination and questions were repeated. Every time I would tell him that I was a Seventh-day Adventist, he would grunt.

When Dr. Danette returned the next morning, he made straight for my bed. I believe he thought my healing was a temporary one due, perhaps, to some sort of religious excitement. So he gave me a searching examination. Again he was puzzled after going through the same routine of questioning. He asked me how long I had been a missionary.

"So you are a Seventh-day Adventist, are you?"

"Yes, I am."

Again the doctor went away to surgery, and again he returned. This time I thought I would ask him a question. I said, "Doctor, I feel well and fit. May I have the privilege of sitting up?"

He said, "This is the sixth day since your accident. I have never known, in all my experience as a medical man, of a pelvic fracture like yours, a compound fracture with all its complications—I've never known the patient to ask to sit up on the sixth day."

Calling the head nurse, he told her that at about lunchtime I was to sit up for fifteen minutes. At suppertime I was allowed to do the same.

The next morning after two more examinations, I asked if I could have another X-ray. He refused, saying it was nonsense to think of it. I asked him if there was a perfect union of the bones. He looked at me and repeated that searching question, "Who are you?" When I told him there was the usual grunt, and he walked away.

After the doctor's next surgery, upon my request, he consented to another X-ray. I also asked permission to stand up at the side of my bed. The X-ray showed a complete, perfect union of all the bones. That afternoon I was allowed to stand for five minutes.

There was still discoloration from my neck to my hips that took several weeks to disappear, but there was never a moment of pain in connection with it.

The next day I was allowed to walk, with the aid of the nurse, to the door. On the ninth or tenth day of my stay in the hospital I was allowed to go home. Clara and I took a berth on a train and went back to Singapore. There we thanked God and gave Him the praise.

The following Sabbath I stepped onto the platform, still with my crutches, which I was told to use for a month. It was an order I obeyed to an extent. While I was preaching, I put my crutches down and walked up and down the platform.

It was wonderful to be healed, but even more thrilling to get back my congregation, which was now on fire for God.

Chapter 29
Through Death's Door

This story of the last-minute healing of a typhoid patient, appeared in *Guide* on February 10, 1971. It was written by Esther Palmer Nuernberger who was a niece of the patient. The author has added this note at the end:

"This is a true story. Della was my aunt. Jessie was my mother. This experience was very precious to Aunt Della. She told it to me many times. To the Fish family, faith was very real and living."

The family farmhouse was buzzing with activity, for this was the day that Lee and Della were to return from their honeymoon. They would stay with Della's parents for just a few days before moving into their own house nearby.

Della was a nurse. She trained at the Battle Creek Sanitarium and Hospital in Battle Creek, Michigan, and had remained there for a few years to work after graduation. Her husband, Lee Canaday, grew up on a neighboring farm in Nebraska.

Della had just finished a long case of private duty before her wedding. Her patient died after a long battle with typhoid fever, a common and serious illness at the turn of the century. Thanks to vaccination and the work of the Public Health Department, this disease is seldom heard of in the United States today.

Della's younger sister, Jessie, was sweeping off the front porch when she saw a cloud of dust down the road. As she looked closer she saw that it was preceded by a team of horses hitched to a spring wagon (a two-seated, open buggy). She recognized it as belonging to her new brother-in-law. But there was only one person riding in the seat! Jessie threw down her broom and ran to the gate. "Where's Della?" she called excitedly.

"She isn't feeling well. I made a bed for her in the bottom of the wagon," Lee answered, "Go and get Pa or Herman to help me carry her into the house."

Jessie was off in a flash and brought her brother Herman. Ma Fish had the covers turned back in Della's own bed, and helped her slip between clean, cool sheets, which felt refreshing to her feverish body. Her auburn hair lay loosely about her face on the pillow, and her freckles stood out plainly against the flushed skin of her face.

As soon as she had rested a few minutes, she called for her father and mother to come to her bedside. Lee was standing beside her when they came into the room. She looked at them and said very solemnly, "Pa, Ma, I'm very much afraid that I have typhoid fever. I think you should send for Dr. Smith."

When the doctor arrived he confirmed Della's suspicions. It was typhoid fever. Under the doctor's directions, they set up the best isolation technique known at the time. Lee was the one to take care of her. Other members of the family came only as close as the open bedroom door.

Day after day dragged by, and Della grew more pale and much weaker. One day when Dr. Smith came to see her, he told the family that she did not have long to live. Della, experienced in the care of typhoid patients, was well aware of her condition.

For many years the Fish family had observed morning and evening worship. The family gathered together for prayer and Bible study at these worship periods. Their faith in God was very real and practical. Each morning and evening the family had not failed to ask God to heal her if it was His will. Della herself had often prayed for the healing of her sick patients, and while she lay on her own bed of sickness, she didn't forget the great Healer, who healed so many while here upon earth.

After Dr. Smith's visit, each member of the family took turns coming to the doorway for a few moments. Della nodded her head in recognition, but was too weak to speak to them. After the last one had come, she lay looking out the window and watching the sunset. As she gazed at the lovely pink and gold sky she whispered a prayer to the One she knew so well. Her prayer was short and simple: "O God, forgive all my sins. If it is Thy will, heal me. Amen."

Then suddenly—and Della never tired of recounting that moment—the whole room was filled with light. At the foot of her bed stood a beautiful, glorious being. In a soft, musical voice he spoke to her and said, "Daughter, your sins are forgiven and you are made whole." As soon as the words were spoken He vanished.

Soon her husband Lee came back into the room, his eyes red from weeping. Della said, "Don't cry, I'm going to get well." And then she told her experience. "Would you please bring me some food and tell the rest of the family to come in?"

Della sat up in bed and ate a hearty meal while the family looked on. The next day she was up and dressed, free from her fever and weakness, a living miracle.

As Dr. David Duffie lay dying of Bubonic Plague, his wife, Martha, was called away on an emergency. Expecting the worst on her return, she opened the door anxiously. There stood David, fully dressed, stethoscope in hand, ready to see patients.

Chapter 30
Healed From Bubonic Plague

World War II was over. Dr. David Duffie and his young wife, Frances, accepted their first mission assignment at a hospital in Peru, the land of cold winds, high plateaus, and llamas.

Peru had experienced occasional outbreaks of bubonic plague such as had swept through Western Europe in the fourteenth and fifteenth centuries. The plague at that time destroyed nearly half of the population. This disease is caused by the bite of fleas, which have previously bitten diseased rats. A human who contracted the plague would usually be dead within a month or less without treatment. Therefore the hospital in Lima, Peru, usually kept a good supply of the necessary medicines from America.

This incredible story of Dr. Duffie's healing was published in the April 20, 1965, issue of *The Youth's Instructor* under the title "Through the Shadows." Martha Duffie wrote the story as her mother, Frances, had told it to her.

"Bubonic plague! You don't think it's bubonic plague, do you, David?" A nameless terror gripped my heart at the very thought. Too well I remembered the tragic role this dread disease had played in the Lopez family as, one by one, all nine members had been carried away to the little hill cemetery. No! This could not be happening to us! Not to my David!

My young doctor husband groaned and painfully turned over in bed. His face was flushed from the high fever, which was now in its second day. "Would you like a drink of water?" I asked.

He nodded. His parched lips eagerly sipped the cooling moisture and then moved to ask, "Did you look up under bubonic plague? What does it say?"

The large medical book in my hands seemed to take on added weight as I slid a finger down the index and fumbled the pages to the place. With trembling voice I read the fine print describing the disease.

"Bubonic plague may be carried by infected rodents," the book read. "Incubation period, one to six days... onset of illness is sudden, usually accompanied by high fever... The first swelling appears in the lymph nodes nearest site of inoculation... Generalized swelling throughout the lymphatic system follows... Disease is endemic to the Titicaca area..."

Quickly we thought back. Last Monday David had finally secured permission to remove medical books from the rat-infested warehouse in Puno. These books had been stored there for months, along with the rest of our things, waiting to be cleared through customs.

Friday afternoon, five days after the Puno trip, David noticed a slight swelling under his left armpit. He did not, however, particularly notice a certain scratch on his left hand. He thought nothing of the swelling.

That evening he had a temperature of 104 degrees. Even that he brushed aside as probably just a bad case of the flu. By Saturday night the "slight swelling" under his arm had enlarged into a painful bubo the size of an egg, and there was considerable swelling all over.

It was then that David first noticed the tiny telltale scratch on his hand. He remembered the rat-infested warehouse, and suspected bubonic plague. Thus far the symptoms matched the description with startling exactness. "But it can't be bubonic plague!" I thought wildly. "It just can't be!"

"If we had a guinea pig we could be sure," David sighed wearily and turned away, too sick to think about it any further.

Through stinging tears I read on—silently now. "A crisis to be reached fifth or sixth day after onset of illness... Can expect either improvement or turn for the worse... Little hope after patient is in coma stage... Coma deepens until death."

I already knew the course of bubonic plague, and that it was usually fatal! I read on: "Sulfadizine in large doses sometimes helpful... Antibubonic serum, if given early in the course of the disease."

Of course! Antibubonic serum! Hope kindled into rapid thought. I fairly leaped to my feet. We would start sulfa at once. We would cable Lima for the serum. Dr. Potts would come from Lima. Everything would be all right! I hurried out to find our trusted, resourceful Noel, the Argentine nurse who was our right-hand helper.

"Bubonic plague!" he gasped. "It can't be! Not our doctor!"

"Well, if we had a guinea pig, we could know for sure," I repeated almost mechanically.

"A guinea pig we'll have," Noel cried, and dashed away, returning a few minutes later with a fat little creature that he had "borrowed" from an understanding, accommodating neighbor. Following David's careful instructions, we took a syringe, removed a small amount of fluid from the largest swelling, and injected it into the abdomen of the guinea pig. The little animal was then carefully DDT'd and kept in a safe place.

While we waited on the results of our guinea pig test, we prepared the cablegram: "Dr. Duffie. Bubonic plague," it read. "Send antibubonic serum. Urgent. Please reply."

Then we anxiously waited. We waited for the serum to come. We waited for the fever to drop. We waited for our other doctor to arrive. We waited for the outcome of the guinea pig's inoculation.

"Has a handcar been sent up from Arequipa?" I inquired at the station late Sunday evening. The railroad operator shook his head. "No, Senora," he replied, "we have no word."

Monday morning I checked again at the station for the medicine, and at the telegraph office for the requested reply. There was no medicine and no reply. "Perhaps it has been necessary to send to the States for the serum," I reasoned. "Surely it will come tonight."

Monday night, no word. Tuesday morning, still no word. This was now the fourth day since the beginning of the illness. David was restless and unable to sleep. I administered the sulfa as the book suggested. I applied the fomentations and rubs. But the fever remained high and the pain unrelieved.

Tuesday afternoon, however, there seemed to be a change. David was quieter and in much less pain than before. He could sleep some too. Thinking he had passed the crisis, we were very happy. Perhaps it wasn't bubonic plague after all. We checked once more on our little guinea pig to see if it was still all right.

But if there seemed to be a small change in the patient's condition, there was a decided change in the guinea pig's, and it was not for the better! The little animal, limp and swollen, was obviously moribund. As we tried to correlate this with the doctor's apparent improvement, it suddenly occurred to us that, instead of improving, David was slipping into a coma. This accounted for his great sleepiness and freedom from pain. At first, the sleep was transitory but as the lapses became more and more pronounced, it became more and more difficult to awaken him.

Deciding at last that the first cablegram had been lost en route to Lima, we sent another. This time we paid twenty soles instead of the usual three, making certain that the cablegram would be delivered to Dr. Potts' home and signed for.

(The first cablegram, we later found, was never received. The second, sent out Wednesday morning, was promptly delivered to the home of Dr. Potts, was received and signed for at the door by the maid. Dr. Potts was not home, however, and the maid placed the urgent cablegram in the top dresser drawer where it was discovered by the doctor two days later.)

Wednesday morning David was unable to take food or to swallow. When aroused, he would mutter incoherently, close his eyes again, and drop back to "sleep." Soon he was completely unconscious.

The guinea pig died that morning, his little abdomen swollen with great bubos. After having Noel dispose of it in the incinerator, I returned, sick at heart, to David's bedside.

At 2:00 p.m. the clinic personnel assembled for special prayer. Then Noel's little Ford pulled out of the compound and made its way down the rough road toward Chullunquiani, our secondary school seven kilometers away. He would bring a group of ministers and teachers back for the planned anointing and prayer service.

I was sitting at the bedside at two o'clock, scarcely able to discern David's breathing, when I noticed that fluid was beginning to form on his lungs. In the darkness of that hour, a phrase from the twenty-third psalm flashed into my mind. "Though I walk through the valley of the shadow of death, I will fear no evil; for thou art with me."

"Is God with me in this hour?" I thought in despair. "Does He hear? Why, oh, why has He not sent help?"

Suddenly there was a knock at the door. When I answered, I found Marcilino standing there with an emergency call from the clinic. A patient was hemorrhaging, he said. Noel had left for the school and wanted me to come at once.

Leaving the boy to sit by the bed with his hand on David's pulse, I gave instructions for him to report instantly if there was any change. Then I hurried out.

The emergency proved to be very serious, and took much longer than expected.

Rushing into the house forty-five minutes later, I found Marcilino sitting on the sofa in the living room, nonchalantly leafing through a *National Geographic* magazine.

My indignation was aroused at this seeming disregard for instructions. One moment I was indignant, and the next terrified at the implications. Why was he in the living room? Had the moment come in my absence? Had Marcilino misunderstood and failed to call me?

The usually dependable Marcilino seemed utterly mystified at my outbreak of emotion, and hesitatingly gave answer to my agonizing queries as to why he had deserted the doctor.

"The doctor told me to go out," he said simply.

"The doctor told you?" I choked back. "The doctor hasn't spoken for two days!" Unable to say another word I tremblingly pushed open the closed door, fearing what

I would find.

The bed was empty. In front of the dresser stood David, fully dressed, stethoscope in hand.

"David Duffie, what are you doing?" I gasped.

"Oh, I thought I'd better go over to the clinic and make rounds," he answered pleasantly. "Haven't seen the patients for several days, have I? What day is it anyway?"

So it was that when the troubled and prayerful little group of teachers arrived at three o'clock for the anointing service, they were ushered into the clinic consultation room for a season of thanksgiving. At the desk sat Dr. Duffie. A look at Marcilino's careful notes said: "2:20, doctor turned over in bed. 2:25, he asked me what I wanted and told me I could go."

At 2:20 the little Ford had reached Chullunquiani, and on hearing the sad news of the seriousness of Dr. Duffie's condition, the men had dropped to their knees in earnest prayer in preparation for the anointing service. It was while these brethren were in prayer that God chose to heal Dr. Duffie.

What a wonderful manifestation of God's love and power, when we earnestly seek Him in prayer.

Chapter 31
Called on God

His nine-year old daughter was dying from bulbar-type poliomyelitis. She was healed, completely and suddenly. She lived for many more years in perfect health. The story, written by Robert W. Link, appeared in the July 1955 issue of *These Times*.

We were vacationing in Minnesota when Bettye, our nine-year-old blond, blue-eyed daughter, came into the cabin from playing down by the lakeshore. We noticed that she didn't look like her sparkling self. Mrs. Link was quick to notice that Bettye was running a fever, and suggested that she lie down on the couch. We were not alarmed, thinking that she probably had an upset stomach, or possibly the start of a summer cold. We treated her accordingly.

It was time for us to leave the lake, and Bettye was still not well. She was still running a low fever, and her stomach was still upset. We returned to Minneapolis, and that night we noticed that she was having a hard time swallowing even water. The next morning her fever increased, and we detected a nasal quality to her voice. When she took a drink of water, she said, "Look, Mommy, the water won't go down; it comes out of my nose."

This was an unusual sign, and we immediately called a pediatrician. He came out to the house; and after a short examination told us the terrible news. Bettye had the dreaded bulbar-type poliomyelitis. He immediately made arrangements for her admittance into the world-famous Sister Kenny Institute in Minneapolis.

You can imagine how my wife and I felt! This disease is sometimes fatal within twenty-four hours. Sometimes paralysis sets in and the victim is hopelessly crippled forever. Doctors must wait a period of several days to determine the correct procedure as far as treatment is concerned.

We knew that we had done all that we could. She had the best that the medical profession could offer, and she was in a hospital where the attendants had the most experience of any in the world. Now all that was left was to wait! Or was that all?

We finally came to our senses after the terrible initial shock. Mrs. Link and I, along with our son Bobby, decided that we had not done all that we could. We knelt on our knees and asked God to look down on poor little Bettye in the hospital. She was, by this time, out of her head, gasping for breath. Her respiratory system was already partially paralyzed.

We were unable to visit Bettye in the isolation ward, and we felt helpless; but somehow we knew that there was Someone with her, and that if it was His will, she would receive comfort and strength from Him.

Friday came. That Sabbath evening we decided to call my superior in the ministry and ask him to get in touch with all the churches in that area (I was located in Chicago at that time) and ask the pastors to have a special prayer for Bettye during the church services.

The next morning, Sabbath morning, Mrs. Link, Bobby, and I again prayed, asking God to be near Bettye. She was by this time unconscious, with a fever of over 105 degrees, and the report the doctor gave us was that she was a very sick little girl. Only God could help her now, although they were getting ready to do a tracheotomy and put her in an iron lung. We read many comforting texts of Scripture, but the one that seemed to give the most help was James 1:6, 7. We knew that if we asked in faith, God would definitely answer our prayers. It gave us courage! We knew that God loved Bettye, and we left all in His hands.

At approximately twelve thirty, just a few minutes after church time, the Elizabeth Kenny Institute called. The head doctor said that he couldn't understand it, but for some reason Bettye's temperature had dropped almost instantly from over 105 degrees to normal!

There it was! God had stepped in and taken over! This was, without a doubt, the most thrilling direct answer to prayer that we had ever seen. The doctor told us later that the only answer that he could give was that someone had been doing some praying.

Bettye improved rapidly from then on. Now she is a healthy, beautiful girl, faithful to her Lord, and anxiously waiting for His coming to this earth. It was the thrill of my life to have the experience of baptizing her recently, and Mrs. Link and I can't thank God enough for the wonderful miracle, which He performed in our behalf!

Chapter 32
The Healing of Nondis

This story appeared in the *Quiet Hour Echoes* (July 1978). This little monthly magazine is put out by the *Quiet Hour* radio broadcast, which is produced by the Tucker family in Redlands, California. LaVerne Tucker also reported his visit to see Nondis in Papua New Guinea after Nondis began working as a physiotherapist.

A breathless messenger burst into Bela village with news of the approaching government patrol. The people, never having seen white men before, fled in terror. Mothers scooped up their babies, and young and old alike fled into the bush and up the slopes of the mountain.

Unaware of the panic-stricken exodus, the patrol officers and their line of carriers trudged wearily into the village only to find empty houses, unattended cooking fires, and Nondis. The young lad, immobilized with crippling leprosy, cringed as an officer with canvas jungle boots and a broad Australian hat bent over him and examined his disease-deformed body.

Within the week, Nondis, who knew nothing of the rest of the world, found himself aboard an airplane en route from Mendi in the Southern Highlands to a leprosarium in Madang on the coast.

Imagine, if you can, the trauma of his experience. A helpless cripple, he is plucked out of his village, away from his family, and flown to a totally different climate where he is sealed in plaster from the soles of his feet to the tops of his hips.

Having no friends and no one who can understand his language, he sits alone on his bed day by day. He is surrounded by a screen to give him the privacy he needs but doesn't want. Nondis was unable even to feed or wash himself because his deformed hands and arms were twisted up against his left shoulder. He depended on others to perform these basic functions.

It was in this condition that Pastor Lew Grieve (then president of the Madang Mission) found Nondis. Thank God for men of compassion. Pastor Grieve brought him food and shirts and, as Nondis slowly learned to speak pidgin, the pastor taught him the basic elements of the gospel. He told Nondis about Jesus, who restored the paralytics and healed the lepers. He said that this Jesus is the same yesterday, today, and forever. Nondis believed.

Three months after being put in plaster, Nondis was cut free. His left leg was badly ulcerated, and his joints were still weak and twisted. It was a terrible disappointment for all. After further treatment he was again sealed in plaster, as before, this time for six months' duration. Pastor Grieve encouraged him to trust in Jesus. Nondis continued to pray without ceasing.

On the second Monday night after being re-encased in plaster, Nondis had a visitor. He dreamed that a tall man in shining white stood by his bed and said to him,

"Nondis, it's time for you to get out of bed."

"I can't," Nondis replied, "Look at me!"

"You can!" the man insisted kindly. "Give me your hand."

Nondis offered a wasted hand with fingers clawed by advanced leprosy.

"Now," said the man. "Open your fingers like this," showing Nondis his open hand.

"It's not possible. You see my nerves have died and my hand is permanently disfigured."

"If you take my hand your own will straighten," he was told.

And it was so.

The man in white then bade Nondis to open and close each hand several times, demonstrating with his own hands as he spoke. Nondis complied. Taking Nondis by the hand the visitor then said, "Now come on, out of bed you get."

In his dream Nondis swung his legs over the side of his hospital bed and stood up.

"Go for a walk," he was told.

He strode off down the ward.

"You have been sick a long time since you first believed," the man said to Nondis when he returned to his bed, "yet your belief in me hasn't wavered at all. Tonight I have taken away your leprosy and have restored your movement. I now want you to work for me."

Nondis said that he would do so, and thanked the man profusely as he turned and went out.

Towards dawn Nondis aroused himself to pray. In the midst of prayer he recalled his dream. Opening his eyes he looked at his hands and was amazed to find his fingers had straightened. Hardly daring to believe what he saw, he clenched and opened his hands several times, marveling at the ease with which he could now move his fingers.

With racing pulse he examined and moved his formerly twisted arms. Next he felt for his legs and was shocked to find the plaster crumbled away. Removing the stocking he ran his hands over each leg in turn, noticing that his sores had healed and that his joints were strong and firm. Overwhelmed with gratitude, he slipped out of bed and for the first time in his life he knelt for prayer, and poured out his thanks to the Lord who had healed him.

On rising to his feet he began to wonder what the reaction of the hospital staff would be on finding him without his plaster on. Afraid that he would be accused of willfully removing it, he again knelt in prayer to ask the Lord to help him convince the staff that he was indeed innocent of this misdemeanor.

The night nurse passed by, so Nondis hesitatingly called out to him and showed him his arms and legs. The nurse, astounded at the sight of a restored Nondis standing before him, called out to the other patients who crowded around talking excitedly. Some loudly denounced Nondis for removing his plaster, and he was disturbed by their accusations.

Finally, Doctor Gilisey was called. Without argument he immediately dismissed the suggestion that Nondis had removed the plaster himself. The doctor reminded those who stood around that this would have been utterly impossible for Nondis in his former condition as he wasn't even capable of feeding himself. Taking Nondis' hand, he carefully examined his fingers, which, in spite of many hours of being massaged with oil by the physiotherapist, had refused to open. Now they were supple and straight.

"I think your God has had something to do with this, Nondis," he said. "I would like to X-ray your legs."

After the X-rays had been taken, the negatives were hung up beside those taken eight days earlier. The difference was discernible at once. In the former the joints were disfigured. In the latter everything appeared as it should.

"There is just one more test I want to do, Nondis," said Dr. Gilisey. He took samples of blood from Nondis' ear lobes, hips, eyebrows, and arm. These were examined under a powerful microscope to see if the leprosy virus was still present. All the tests were negative.

Doctor Russell, from Port Moresby was responsible for discharging safe lepers. He gave Nondis an unqualified clearance to return home. Nondis then approached Dr. Gilisey and told him of the commission he had been given in his dream:

"The Lord said I should work for Him, but I really don't know what kind of work I should do," he said. "Can you give me some work?"

The doctor put Nondis to work in the physiotherapy department under the tutorship of the chief physiotherapist, Mrs. Hamilton. After receiving his certificate in 1967 he requested a transfer to an Adventist hospital. Dr. Gilisey arranged with Mr. Alan Stiles, the O. I. C. at the Togoba Adventist Leprosarium, for Nondis to work there under Mr. Earl Hokin.

While at Togoba, Nondis was baptized and married by Pastor Harold Harker. His wife, Rebecca, is a lovely Christian woman. Later Nondis transferred to the Seventh-day Adventist hospital at Hatzfeldhaven.

In 1973 Nondis was given the opportunity for further training in his profession in Port Moresby. Although he had no schooling at all, he taught himself enough to compete favorably with other physiotherapy students who had completed the fourth form. At the conclusion of his course he received his second certificate and was asked if he would take an appointment at Mendi hospital. Eager to return to his home area he accepted.

In May of 1978 I watched John Nondis at work for Jesus. He was lovingly ministering as a physiotherapist to the hundreds of needy people who came to the Mendi Hospital in the highlands of western Papua New Guinea. I took those hands in my own—hands that were once so grotesque and twisted, but now through the mighty healing power of Jesus are able to massage and soothe aching bodies. I held them up for all to see.

John said, "Jesus along time He come help me. Heal me."

I asked, "Did He heal you completely so doctors could find no trouble—no more leprosy?"

John said, "Yes."

My response was, "Wonderful! Isn't Jesus wonderful?"

Worshipfully John responded, "Yes, Jesus wonderful!"

We invite you to view the complete
selection of titles we publish at:

www.TEACHServices.com

Scan with your mobile
device to go directly
to our website.

Please write or e-mail us your praises, reactions, or
thoughts about this or any other book we publish at:

www.TEACHServices.com • (800) 367-1844

P.O. Box 954
Ringgold, GA 30736

info@TEACHServices.com

TEACH Services, Inc., titles may be purchased in bulk for
educational, business, fund-raising, or sales promotional use.
For information, please e-mail:

BulkSales@TEACHServices.com

Finally, if you are interested in seeing
your own book in print, please contact us at

publishing@TEACHServices.com

We would be happy to review your manuscript for free.

www.ingramcontent.com/pod-product-compliance
Lightning Source LLC
Chambersburg PA
CBHW081923170426
43200CB00014B/2817